CW00337116

Cheshire Churches

A guide to the ancient parish churches of the county, 1066 to 1820

by

Roland W. Morant

To GWYNETH

Acknowledgements

To the work of F.H. Crossley for providing analyses of the architectural development of many of the churches; to the authors of individual church guidebooks and to Pevsner's "Cheshire" for building dates, and names of architects and builders; to Dr. N. Ball for help and advice on the history of Christianity in Cheshire; and to incumbents and parochial church councils who endeavour to keep their churches open to visitors or who provide information on where keys may be borrowed. *R.W.M.*

First published 1989 by Countyvise Limited, 1 & 3 Grove Road, Rock Ferry, Birkenhead, Wirral, Merseyside L42 3XS.

Copyright © Roland W. Morant, 1989.

Photoset and printed by Birkenhead Press Limited, 1 & 3 Grove Road, Rock Ferry, Birkenhead, Merseyside L42 3XS.

ISBN 0 907768 18 0.

All rights reserved. No part of this publication may be reproduced, stored in a retrieval system, or transmitted, in any form, or by any means, electronic, chemical, mechanical, photocopying, recording or otherwise, without the prior permission of the publisher.

Contents

Foreword

To obtain information about old churches, most visitors rely on being able to purchase a small booklet on sale inside the entrance to the building. Often such information, if available, is sparse or uneven in quality, or is the 'Nth' reprint of material that was first written many years ago. For those churches where brief literature is not on sale, visitors may be obliged to turn to general descriptive books which are sometimes too bulky for ready reference or carrying around. For Cheshire there are two general works that should be mentioned: Raymond Richards' "Old Cheshire Churches", now sadly out of print but found on the reference shelves of most of the county's public libraries, gives details of nearly all the ancient parish churches and other chapels, etc. In the Buildings of England series, Pevsner's "Cheshire" offers succinctly presented information on churches which is sandwiched between descriptions of other public as well as domestic buildings.

This guidebook has been written to meet the need for a small and compact volume which will afford quick reference for visitors. It therefore contains specific information on all the old parish churches of Cheshire, besides some more general introductory information about the history of Christianity in Cheshire and the development of ecclesiastical architecture in the county. "Parish churches" is the term taken here to include all church-buildings including chapels of the Established Church which are open or were formerly open for public worship; "Old" refers to all those parish churches that were first built before the end of George III's reign in 1820; while "Cheshire" without additional qualification is used to mean the pre-1974 county which was, except for one or two minor instances, co-terminous with the present diocese of Chester.

Though constructed after 1820, Birtles parish church is included because of the many ancient artefacts it contains. Two other churches, Northenden and Holt, are also described in this guidebook since for much of their history and indeed until fairly recently they formed part of the diocese of Chester.

1. INTRODUCTION

Looking at Cheshire on the map, we see that it forms an inverted triangle between the mountains of Clwyd in the west and the Peak District in the east. Along the hypotenuse of this triangle to the north is the River Mersey and its estuary leading to the Irish Sea; while at the blunt apex of the triangle to the south is the flattish and less readily identifiable area which is continuous with the northern extremities of Shropshire and Staffordshire. Because of its key geographical location in the north west of England, the Cheshire plain has long been used as a route by travellers journeying between London and Scotland, or between eastern England and North Wales etc. The recent construction of the M6 motorway which slices through Cheshire, has helped to perpetuate a longstanding attitude that Cheshire is seen as a part of the country to pass through and not as a destination in its own right. Indeed as Pevsner remarked a few years ago, "Cheshire is not a county much visited by architectural travellers. Nor is it often the specific goal of tourists . . . it is one of the least known of English counties"[1].

Things, though, are changing. Anyone strolling along Eastgate Street in Chester or across the Square in Nantwich in the height of Summer will bear witness to the throngs of tourists visiting Cheshire's towns. Though the county now may be more frequently visited, there is little doubt that collectively and individually the parish churches — save for a few — remain little known. Most people are aware of the glorious towers of Somerset churches or the majestic exterior appearances of the churches of Gloucestershire or Yorkshire, but how many people can visualise the churches of Cheshire?

It is probably not coincidental that some recent writers of books on English churches (such as E. Smith, O. Cook & G. Hutton in their "English Parish Churches"[2] or R. Foster in his "Discovering English Churches"[3]) have tended to be fleeting in their aesthetic or architectural appreciation of Cheshire churches. It is tempting to conclude that their omission is due to lack of knowledge rather than because the churches of the county generally lack interest or beauty. If the latter is the reason, it was not shared by Alec Clifton-Taylor, one of the most authoritative experts on English ecclesiastical architecture. In his book, "English Parish Churches as Works of Art"[4], he noted that the county has a number of buildings of considerable distinction.

It cannot be denied that the friable quality of the sandstone of which almost all the medieval churches in Cheshire have been constructed, has both inhibited their design and ornamentation, and detracted from their present external appearance, chiefly through loss in detail and because of a darkening effect, both due to weathering. The main attraction tends to be church interiors with particular reference to the embossed and panelled camber-beam roofs, the ornamental timber screens, and the warm pink and red colouring of the stonework. During the first half of the present century, Fred Crossley published a series of articles in local antiquarian journals[5] in which he described in detail the subtle and restrained beauties of the medieval churches of the county, and there seems little doubt to the present writer that his powerful advocacy was correct.

Compared with other counties such as Norfolk which has more than six hundred medieval churches, Cheshire does not possess the sheer concentration of ecclesiastical buildings from which those of merit might be selected. However, few visitors to the county wanting to become acquainted with its churches would reject the claims, say of Nantwich, Astbury or Malpas, to be ecclesiastical buildings of the highest quality and well capable of standing comparison with the best in the country.

---

[1]Pevsner, N. & Hubbard, E. (1971) *Cheshire* (Harmondsworth: Penguin), p.11.
[2]Smith, E., Cook, O. & Hutton, G. (1976) *English parish churches* (London: Thames and Hudson)
[3]Foster, R. (1981) *Discovering English churches* (London: BBC)
[4]Clifton-Taylor, A. (1974) *English parish churches as works of art* (London: Batsford), p.240
[5]Referred to later in the section on "Further Reading".

2. Early Christianity in Cheshire

During Roman times Chester was a strategic military base, but probably not an ecclesiastical centre. However, it is likely that there were some Christians among the military and civilian population of the city. The legions departed from Britain in 410, and from this time for approximately two centuries there was mounting chaos throughout the land. Gradually the north, east and central parts of what is now England were overrun and subdued by the heathen Angles. Cheshire, as much affected by the chaos as anywhere else in central England, was absorbed into the Anglian kingdom of Mercia c.600.

How Cheshire was converted (or reconverted) to Christianity is highly speculative. It is known that the main task of converting heathen Mercia including Cheshire fell to the Northumbrian Christians based at Lindisfarne (Holy Isle). Led by the Scot Diuma, they visited Mercia c.653 and baptised Peada the son of the heathen king Penda. In 669 Chad who had relinquished the see of York to Wilfrid, was appointed bishop of Mercia with his episcopal seat at Lichfield. Thenceforth for two hundred and fifty years, successive bishops of this Mercian diocese had the episcopal oversight of Cheshire. This control was loose as the area of the present county facing North Wales was a frontier district frequently fought over by Anglian and Welsh chieftains. Until Cheshire became firmly incorporated into the diocese of Lichfield in 920, it was in reality a missionary area.

A number of ancient churches in Cheshire are dedicated to Northumbrian holy men of C7, suggesting this earlier connection. Thus churches dedicated to St. Chad include: Chadkirk, Farndon, Holt (now in Clwyd), Over, Tushingham and Wybunbury. Those to St. Wilfrid include: Davenham, Grappenhall, Mobberley and Northenden. St. Oswald, king of Northumbria, is honoured in the dedications of the churches of Backford, Bidston, Brereton, Lower Peover and Malpas, and the south transept of the cathedral. The Northumbria/Mercia connection is also indicated by the presence of fragments of crosses of Mercian design at various places in the county.

It is likely too that later action in bringing Cheshire to the Christian Faith was undertaken in the Wirral in C9 and C10 by separate groups of Irish and Norse settlers arriving from Ireland

and/or the Isle of Man. Probably, the Irish settlers came earlier than the Norsemen. The influence of these groups is suggested by two kinds of evidence. Thus several churches in Wirral and Chester have dedications pointing to a possible connection: At West Kirby there is St. Bridget and at Wallasey, St. Hilary; while in Chester there are St. Bridget (the church was destroyed in C19) and St. Olave (Olaf). The other evidence comprises fragments of wheel-shaped crosses of Irish or Isle of Man influence located at several sites in Wirral.

Cheshire continued to be politically unstable for much of the second half of the first millenium and because it was frequently fought over during this period, many districts became "no man's lands". This situation coupled with the fact that much of Cheshire was covered at the time by forest, explains why a tight pattern of parishes failed to be established until after the Norman Conquest, except in Wirral and, possibly, down the east bank of the River Dee.

Accordingly, the missionary scheme operated by the Mercian diocese based on Lichfield involved the conjectural foundation of a number of minsters of which three might have been at Chester, Sandbach and Prestbury. A minster's physical presence would have been marked in its early days by a large cross, and later by a church. A team of priests would have served the minster and its surrounding area. It may well be that these minsters which were small in number with each having an oversight of a large area, were the forerunners of the multi-township parishes which characterised Cheshire and other parts of the north of England in later medieval days.

3. The Church in the Middle Ages and Afterwards

Little is known of the state of Christianity in the final Anglo-Saxon period, that is immediately before the Norman Conquest of 1066. It is probable that there were a few small churches dispersed throughout the county owing allegiance to the diocese of Lichfield. A few years after the Conquest, William I in pacifying the north, passed through Cheshire in 1069-70 and laid waste many of the habitations in the east and south of the county. It is therefore probable that some if not all of the Anglo-Saxon churches that there were in these districts, were made derelict by the Norman soldiery. Though not altogether reliable as a factual account, Domesday Book records the general picture involving the parishes prior to 1086, the year of its formulation. The book names three churches in Chester, nine parishes in the remainder of Cheshire with churches, and fourteen other parishes with priests. These three lists taken together indicate how few parishes, churches and priests there must have been in early Norman Cheshire.

The policy of the Norman rulers was to locate diocesan centres in large towns, rather than in small towns or villages which had often been the Anglo-Saxon practice. Thus the see for the old Lichfield diocese was moved in 1075 from that town to St. John Baptist at Chester. Here it remained for just twenty years before being moved once more to Coventry which it came to share with Lichfield as a dual diocesan centre. St. John's, Chester, though continuing to retain a nominal and shadowy cathedral status until the Reformation, became a collegiate foundation which was abolished at the Suppression. Cheshire remained part of the extensive diocese of Coventry and Lichfield until 1541 when Henry VIII established a separate diocese of Chester. The seat of the bishop was allotted to the suppressed abbey of St. Werburgh in the city of Chester, the abbey being reconstituted as the cathedral of Christ and the Blessed Virgin Mary.

Until comparatively recently and especially in medieval times, much of Cheshire was covered in forest. This was particularly so in the east where the Forest of Macclesfield spread along the foothills of the Pennines from Stockport to Bosley, and in the north central area where the Forest of Delamere stretched from the River Mersey to Church Minshull. The greatest concentration of ancient parishes and churches lay in the predominantly agricultural districts beyond these forested areas. These districts were the Wirral, Chester and the tract of land a few miles wide on the east side of the River Dee extending from Chester to Farndon and Malpas. A second, lesser concentration of parishes and churches was located in the agricultural area of south and mid Cheshire. Based on the salt-making axis of Nantwich, Middlewich and Northwich, it stretched up towards the River Mersey and divided the Forests of Delamere and Macclesfield.

At the time of Domesday the population of Cheshire was probably as small as 11,000. It gradually increased during the later medieval period in keeping with the stabilising political situation and as the general standard of living improved, though there was a sharp but temporary setback in the aftermath of the Black Death of 1349. The increase in population was matched by the founding of more churches in the county to meet the spiritual needs of the people. By 1540 the year of Henry VIII's Suppression, it is calculated that there were around 130 churches in existence which were open for public worship.

From the early medieval period until early C19, most of Cheshire was divided into large parishes, especially in the forested areas, in which there were a number of townships (i.e. hamlets). Each parish was served by a parish church together with a number of subsidiary or satellite churches called parochial chapels and chapels of ease. A parochial chapel was a foundation where all the functions and rites of its mother parish church could be performed. It was staffed from late medieval times by a chaplain appointed in perpetuity, a functionary who after the Reformation was known as perpetual curate. Right of presentation to the chaplaincy or perpetual curacy rested normally with the patron of the living of the mother church, and the major tithes of the parochial chapel were remitted to the mother church. A chapel of ease, of lower status than a parochial chapel, was used for all religious purposes save the "liberties of public baptism and burial". In every respect save these two, a chapel of ease served as an adjunct to the mother church, the clergy of the latter staffing it. These subsidiary churches were located in the townships, although it often happened that not every small township was served by such a building.

These "multi-township" parishes varied enormously in size. One of the largest, in the Forest of Macclesfield, was Prestbury which at one time contained thirty two townships. Smaller examples included Middlewich with fifteen townships, and

Shotwick with five[1]. Apart from the interruption caused by the Black Death, the populations of townships steadily expanded throughout the Middle Ages and afterwards. As a result, some separate parishes, each consisting of a small number of townships, were hived off from these multi-township parishes especially in C18 and early C19. At the same time — or sometimes after considerable delay — the chapels of such new parishes achieved full parochial status. Instances of these in Cheshire are many, with examples including Congleton (a former chapel of ease of Astbury), Nantwich (a former parochial chapel of Acton) and Witton (a former parochial chapel of Great Budworth).

Until C19 the diocese of Chester took in much of pre-1974 Lancashire as well as portions of Yorkshire and present Clwyd. The rapid increase of population which accompanied the Industrial Revolution in C18 and C19 made it necessary to divide the diocese. Thus the Yorkshire parishes went to Ripon in 1836; its Westmorland and Cumberland parishes were transferred to Carlisle, and its parishes in the north and east of pre-1974 Lancashire to Manchester, all in 1847; the parish of Holt went to St. Asaph in 1861; and its parishes in south west pre-1974 Lancashire were removed to Liverpool in 1880. Finally, Northenden and Wythenshawe were transferred to the diocese of Manchester in C20 to match civil changes affecting these areas. As an outcome of this series of changes, the present diocese of Chester is co-extensive with Cheshire as it existed prior to 1974.

---

[1]For a detailed description, see Sylvester, D. (1967) "Parish and township in Cheshire and North-East Wales" in *Journal of the Chester Archaeological Society*, Vol.54, pp.23-35.

4. Church Dedications

The dedications of ancient churches in Cheshire provide some interesting facts. The saint most commonly venerated is St. Mary the Virgin with twenty six churches named after her. One or two of these may originally have been dedicated to St. Mary Magdalene, but there is no way of distinguishing them today. St. Mary is followed by St. Peter with twelve, St. Michael or St. Michael and All Angels (ten), and All Saints (nine). Although a few of these dedications were given to churches founded after the Reformation (for instance Stockport St. Peter), the frequency of these dedications in Cheshire may be taken as reflecting their popularity throughout the country in medieval times[1].

Why were these saints so popular? St. Mary the Virgin was regarded by people living in the Middle Ages as the supreme intercessor to Our Lord, being especially capable as Mother of approaching her Son on behalf of souls. St. Peter was clearly popular as he held the keys of Heaven and was thus perceived as controlling access to that Place. St. Michael the protector of high places (illustrated admirably at Mottram-in-Longdendale and Wincle) was the destroyer of Evil and the leader in Heaven of the Church Militant. The dedication of All Saints (or, more usually, in pre-Reformation days All Hallows) was regarded as a powerful means of invoking intercessions, that is through the whole company of saints.

There are a few uncommon, single dedications in the county. St. Bertoline who was a Mercian prince about whom little is known, is remembered at Barthomley; while at Bunbury the church is dedicated to St. Boniface (c.680-755), the Devon missionary to the German people. St. Werburgh the Mercian princess to whom Chester abbey (now cathedral) used to be dedicated, gave her name to the church at Warburton. St. Edith of Polesworth, believed to have been a sister of Edward the Elder, is remembered at Shocklach and St. Alban the first British martyr, at Tattenhall[2].

It may not have escaped notice that there are word connections between Bertoline, Boniface and Werburgh on the one hand, and Barthomley, Bunbury and Warburton respectively on the other. But whether each of the saints was chosen as a subject of dedication because of similarity to the existing name of a parish, or whether a parish was named after a saint whose name had been already given to the church in that parish, cannot be established for certain. Interestingly, two other parishes also suggest lingering connections of the same type: Plemstall the church of which is dedicated to St. Peter, was the traditional home or retreat of St. Plegmund who became Archbishop of Canterbury in Alfred's reign; while the church at Swettenham, dedicated in modern times to St. Peter after the ancient dedication had been lost, may have had an earlier dedication to St. Swithun.

There are a few double dedications: St. James and St. Paul at Marton, St. Mary and St. Helen at Neston, St. Mary and St. James at Birkenhead, and St. Mary and All Saints at Great Budworth. One other double dedication of course is at the cathedral. This was conferred in 1541 by Henry VIII, and is to Christ and the Blessed Virgin Mary.

In later medieval times especially, dedications were changed in a number of Cheshire churches, not least for reasons connected with the prevailing popularity of saints notably St. Mary. Among the changed dedications were:—

Bosley	— St. Thomas the Martyr (first) and St. Lawrence (afterwards), now St. Mary the Virgin
Great Budworth	— God and All Saints, now St. Mary and All Saints
Macclesfield	— All Hallows or All Saints, now St. Michael and All Angels
Nether Alderley	— St. Lawrence, now St. Mary
Stockport	— All Hallows, now St. Mary
Taxal	— St. Leonard, now St. James
Thornton-le-Moors	— St. Helen, now St. Mary

In the long period of Protestant ascendancy following the Reformation, the dedications of new churches were nearly always restricted to Biblical saints (such as Hargrave St. Peter or Threapwood St. John), to All Saints (at Somerford) or to Christ (at Alsager and Macclesfield). St. George was selected at Altrincham and Carrington, no doubt for patriotic reasons.

---

[1]See Bond, F. (1914) *Dedications & patron saints of English churches* (London: Oxford University Press), Ch. III, p.17-27 for a full list of saints in rank order of popularity.
[2]The churches dedicated to Northumbrian saints, and saints having an Iro-Norse connection, are referred to in Chapter 2, "Early Christianity in Cheshire".

5. Trends and Influences in the Design and Construction of Churches

For the whole of the medieval period, Cheshire was a remote part of the country. It was many miles from the main centres of influence and power. A journey from London to Chester would have taken a traveller the best part of a week. In his Introduction to Raymond Richards' book, Fred Crossley observed that the closer to the centre of fashion a locality was, the quicker the change. Thus a remote district like Cheshire might have lagged forty or fifty years in implementing new architectural styles[1]. This geographical factor must be kept in mind in comprehending how ecclesiastical modes evolved in the county.

In two periods after the Conquest, architectural styles continued to be used in the county long after they had been discontinued elsewhere. The first of these was the Norman period of C12 when features like the round pier, the cushion capital and the single-stepped semi-circular arch were constructed well on towards the end of that century. The second period was during C14 when the established Decorated style went into rapid decline in many parts of England after the Black Death of 1349. It remained an active architectural force, however, in Cheshire until as late as perhaps 1390. Examples of this prolonged trend include the rebuilding of Astbury tower and spire which occurred not earlier than 1366 (paid for by money left in a will), the reconstruction of Bunbury chancel which started in 1386 under the patronage of Sir Hugh Calveley, and the rebuilding of the north aisle at Acton c.1400 to accommodate the tomb of Sir William Mainwaring.

It is undoubtedly true that the medieval church builders in Cheshire were at times highly conservative in their approach to the work in which they relied on well-tried methods of construction and modes of design. The best example is at Chester cathedral where the south arcade of the nave was rebuilt c.1360 in the Decorated style and the north arcade was rebuilt c.1490 to match this earlier work. In many smaller churches the octagonal pier and capital, with double-chamfered arch, were used in arcade construction over a period lasting from c.1250 to c.1550, another indication of how slow to change were fashions in the county.

If not their conservative instincts, certainly economical attitudes led master-masons throughout the medieval period to re-use or remodel existing features of a building such as a window-frame, doorway or archway — especially if it was constructed of a valuable material or was intricately moulded. An example is found at Bruera where the semi-circular arch of a Norman south doorway was rebuilt in C14 where it incorporated a pointed arch. Another example is the heightening of the C13 Early English nave piers at Acton perhaps two centuries later. A third instance is at Witton where the whole of its C14 north arcade was re-used when the nave was widened in C15/C16. In modern times too, possibly for reasons to do with conservation more than economy, ancient fabric may be sometimes re-employed, as at Woodchurch where a Norman doorway and three C17 windows were retained in 1964-65 when the church was enlarged or at Over where C14 material including the east window of the former chancel was inserted into the new work in 1926 when the building was elongated. Just as when out-of-date architectural styles are used by modern builders, the re-use of old material can lead to many a pitfall in attempting to put an accurate date on a section of a church.

A modest surge in erecting new churches and in rebuilding old in Cheshire, took place in Norman times especially during the mid and later part of C12. It is possible to identify a total of thirty churches (including four with fonts of the period only) that contain, or are recorded as having contained until being destroyed in C19, some Norman work. This impetus in building which was mirrored often more strongly elsewhere in England, was clearly an outcome of the relatively stable situation resulting from the imposed settlement of the Normans. However, there does seem to have been a fall-off in the rate of construction during the greater part of the following (C13) century. Some fifteen churches of this period in the county are known to possess, or to have possessed until C19, Early English fabric. In addition, six other churches can be identified as having late C13 transitional Early English/Decorated work. A likely explanation for this apparent reduction is that during this century manpower and physical resources were being redirected towards fighting offensive wars against the Welsh and in building and strengthening military defences, notably Chester and Beeston castles.

Towards the end of C13 there occurred in Cheshire an event of great importance, namely the founding in 1277 of the great abbey of Vale Royal in the centre of the county. Its patron was Edward I who laid the foundation stone in August of that year in the presence of Bishop Burnell and the Bishop of St. Asaph. Taking at least seventy years to assemble, the abbey consumed great quantities of stone and timber. Put in charge of the work was the king's architect, Master Walter of Hereford, and he supervised the project in its early stages, dying c.1315. We can assume that Walter's close connections with the English court ensured that the abbey was constructed in keeping with the prevalent architectural style (Decorated) of the times. Thus it is thought that he may well have been responsible for bringing the ogee-arch and the Caernarvon or shouldered arch (both commonly employed at Nantwich) to the county. It is known, moreover, that a lodge or school of masons came into being at the abbey carrying on Walter's work long after his death and undertaking commissions in the neighbourhood, for example at several churches such as Backford, Handley, Shotwick and Nantwich (where the work is indicated by masons' marks).

During the first half of C14, there was a surge of church building throughout Cheshire in the new Decorated style. Besides the abbey church of St. Werburgh (now the cathedral), this involved the major churches of Acton, Astbury, Audlem, Bunbury, Frodsham, Great Budworth, Malpas, Middlewich, Nantwich, Over and Witton, as well as many lesser churches. The total number of churches today which can be identified as possessing, or having possessed prior to C19, such Decorated work is forty five. Temporarily halted in 1349 because of the Black Death which at one stroke removed one third of the population including many of the best craftsmen, this Decorated building programme regained its momentum c.1360 and continued in Cheshire until nearly the end of the century, as at Acton, Audlem and Nantwich. There was then a quiescent period which lasted for about seventy five years (i.e. from c.1400 to c.1475). During this long period there was little construction work in stone taking place in the county. It has never been completely explained why in Cheshire, in contrast to some other areas of the country such as East Anglia, this was so. Why did the rate of construction dwindle to a trickle? A speculative answer might be that there was an emphasis at this time for economic reasons on the assembly of small timber-framed churches (for example Holmes Chapel or Siddington), many of which were replaced in C17 or later by stone or brick edifices (such as Harthill, Tushingham, etc.). Only at Gawsworth can work in stone be firmly attributed to the middle of C15. Here, the nave was commenced c.1430 in the new Perpendicular style.

The most exciting period of church building in Cheshire lasted from c.1475 to c.1540 during which a sustained and ambitious programme took place. Granted that a small amount of early

Gawsworth nave, early Perpendicular south window with moderately acute arch, c.1430.

Perpendicular work had been introduced into a few churches in the first part of C15 (such as the south window of the south transept at Nantwich) there came into use a mature style of Perpendicular in the western half of Cheshire that spilled over into that part of present Clwyd that was dominated by the famous Stanley family, and into south Lancashire. Sixty eight churches may be identified in Cheshire which contain Perpendicular work. In addition another six churches can be positively identified as having had Perpendicular work which has now disappeared. The style employed in Cheshire in C15 is believed to have been first brought to the area by masons originating in the Severn valley, a district relatively unravaged by the Black Death.

A question which has been often asked, is "Where did the money come from to pay for this big programme of reconstruction at the end of the medieval period?" One writer, J.T. Driver, suggested in his book "Cheshire in the later middle ages, 1399-1540" that whereas in areas like the Cotswolds or East Anglia funding was provided out of the profits of the wool and textile industries, no clear-cut answer can be given in respect of Cheshire. Possible sources of revenue mentioned by him include the rising income derived from improved land-management, profits from the salt industry in Nantwich and Middlewich, profits of trade and commerce in Chester, and the surplus income of the landed aristocracy and gentry (such as William Troutbeck at Chester St. Mary or Ralph Egerton at Bunbury)[2]. Cheshire at this time was never particularly wealthy, and as Fred Crossley pointed out in his book "Cheshire", rarely could a church be entirely remodelled in the newer fashion (Brereton and Weaverham are exceptions). What often resulted was a delightful blending of C14 and C15 or C16 styles[3] (for instance Astbury or Great Budworth).

About 1540 the spate of church building diminished sharply, but it did not stop entirely. This fall-off was due to the changed religious and political situation brought about by Henry VIII which caused many of the traditional sources of finance for construction and maintenance of ecclesiastical buildings to dry up or be diverted to other, secular ends. The result was that a number of churches remained unfinished, some permanently. The most striking example is Bebington where the chancel, chancel chapels and the first bay of the nave and aisles had been recently rebuilt leaving the whole of the western section in its original pre-C15/C16 condition. Another is Tarvin with only the north aisle and west tower having been rebuilt in the Perpendicular style. Some other churches (such as Holt, Over and Weaverham) apparently failed to receive their new clerestories.

Brereton, St. Oswald.

Some new building or reconstruction did take place in the immediate aftermath of this religious turmoil. The least of this involved a modest patching up so that churches could be used for public worship. As a rule, where a little work would suffice the least expensive and easiest course of action was adopted. Thus at Bebington the east and west ends of the church were crudely united early after the Suppression; while at Bunbury a small clerestory was installed in early Elizabethan times (a clerestory replaced by the present one in C19).

A few major projects which had been commenced before the Suppression, were continued and completed in mid C16. At Over for instance, it is recorded that substantial work was being done in 1543. At Cheadle a long campaign of reconstruction which had started c.1520, was brought to fruition in 1556. A third church where work had been taking place at the time of the Suppression is Disley where the structure was consecrated in 1558.

The Elizabethan Settlement brought a measure of calm and stability, and Elizabeth I's long reign (1558-1603) afforded a period of steadily increasing prosperity. There were in consequence a number of people who wished to devote some of their financial gains in the form of gifts or bequests to the maintenance of the fabric of their local churches. A study of Elizabethan wills suggests that most bequests of the period were intended to meet essential minor repairs to windows, roofs, towers and spires, etc. For the time being, grandiose schemes involving building new churches or rebuilding old were no longer fashionable or practicable. An exception though to this negative trend was the reconstruction of former chantry or oratory chapels as mortuary chapels by the gentry.

The chief recipients of former monastic and other ecclesiastical properties after the Suppression were the peerage and landed gentry. The services of skilled craftsmen formerly employed on church work were in great demand by the upper classes from 1540 onwards. The stonemasons, woodcarvers, carpenters and glaziers were thus increasingly occupied in the adaptation of former church property (such as Combermere and Vale Royal abbeys) and in the construction and beautification of new country and town houses especially in Chester and Nantwich. Not surprisingly such construction work that was undertaken in churches in Elizabethan times tended to be domestic Perpendicular in style.

The picture in the first half of C17 (known as the Jacobean period) tended to be similar to that of the Elizabethan period with repair and maintenance of churches the chief activity, though a small number of churches were rebuilt in the long-lingering

Upper Peover, neo-Classical mortuary chapel, 1648.

domestic Perpendicular style. Cheshire was slow to experiment with the emerging neo-Classical style (used for instance by Inigo Jones at St. Paul's, Covent Garden, 1631-38). Indeed the first church in the county where the new style was employed, was Upper Peover where Ellen Mainwaring built a north chancel mortuary chapel in 1648.

An eleven year interval of time separated the year 1649 when Charles I was executed from 1660 when the monarchy was restored in the person of Charles II. For practical purposes the earlier of these two dates may be taken to mark the termination of a long period starting in early Christian times when all churches were designed to accommodate sacramental worship. Such catholic worship, especially in the later medieval period, necessitated the provision of large chancels, transepts and side-aisles for mass-altars and processions, etc. This traditional form of worship, though severely inhibited by the activities of protestant reformers continued essentially unchanged in later Tudor and Elzabethan times.

However, the long unsettled period following the Reformation and lasting for over a hundred years was brought to a conclusion by the Restoration of the monarchy. This last event confirmed the position of the Church of England as the Established Church, with an emphasis in Anglican churches placed on the preaching of the Word. The pulpit and reading desk, often combined as a "three-decker" and normally placed at the east end of the nave, frequently became the focus of worship at the expense of the chancel and high altar. Accordingly, a main aim in post-Restoration and Georgian days was to transform old churches into protestant preaching houses having the appearance of galleried halls[4]. In the event the majority of existing churches were adapted to this purpose, a few such buildings in Cheshire retaining their C18 character to the present day (such as Congleton). One outcome of the rapid increase in population especially in towns affected by the Industrial Revolution (e.g. Altrincham, Congleton, Macclesfield and Stockport) was that some entirely new churches were built in C18 and a greater number in early C19, all conforming to the preaching house design.

---

[1]Crossley, F.H. (1973) in Richards, R. *Old Cheshire churches* (Manchester: Morten) p.1.
[2]Driver, J.T. (1971) *Cheshire in the later middle ages, 1399-1540* (Chester: Cheshire Community Council) pp.60-61.
[3]Crossley, F.H. (1949) *Cheshire* (London: Robert Hale) pp.176-177.
[4]Discussed in detail in Addleshawe, G.W.O. & Etchells, F. (1948) *The architectural setting of Anglican Worship* (London: Faber).

6. Traditional Building Materials

The greater part of Cheshire consists of a broad plain which is bounded to the north by the River Mersey and its estuary leading to the Irish Sea. To the south the plain continues into Shropshire and Staffordshire where there is a less obvious boundary provided by the Ellesmere Moraine. To the west the Cheshire plain is bordered by the River Dee; while to the east Cheshire terminates in the high hills of the Peak District. Scattered over the Cheshire plain, there are outcrops of soft sandstone of the Keuper type ranging in colour from yellow to red, buff and grey. In addition, especially in the Chester district is found the soft pinkish Bunter sandstone. Both these kinds of rocks have provided from early times a readily available building material for the construction of churches — and nearly all of the surviving ancient ones are constructed of these friable sandstones.

In the Peak District which overlaps the eastern borders of the county are older rocks of the Carboniferous series, and a few churches (notably Astbury and Pott Shrigley) are built of Millstone Grit. The latter is a rock of the Carboniferous which is characterised by being resistant to the weather and normally grey or pale buff in colour. Another Carboniferous sandstone is Kerridge stone which is quarried near Maçclesfield. A traditional roofing material in Cheshire, it is sombre in appearance and is frequently found on the roofs of many churches in the form of exceedingly heavy slabs. During the reign of George III, it tended to be replaced by the thinner and cheaper Welsh slate, a material often used on more modern church roofs.

As already mentioned, much of Cheshire was covered in forest until two or three hundred years ago. Timber was, therefore, very plentiful and was often used in the construction of small medieval churches (such as Baddiley, Marton, Siddington or Warburton Old Church). A number of these timbered edifices were replaced in the period following the Middle Ages by brick and, occasionally, stone buildings (such as Coppenhall, Goostrey or Swettenham). However, the colour of the brick made in the county which varies from a dull grey to an equally insipid red, does not lend distinction to the external appearance of local churches.

7. The Churches and their Architecture

Unlike one or two of its county neighbours such as Shropshire, Cheshire possesses not a single church with Anglo-Saxon fabric *in situ*. There is, however, a scattering of sculptural relics which are found in Wirral and along the eastern side of the county, indicating a wide but thinly spread pre-Conquest Christian presence. Nearly all of these surviving artefacts are fragments of preaching or minster crosses, and boundary or grave crosses.

By far the finest remnants are the two large crosses, re-assembled from broken pieces, which stand in the market square at Sandbach. Of possibly late C8 or early C9 and therefore pre-Scandinavian in date, they display vine scrolls, coarsened interlace, beasts, doll-like heads, and religious scenes in the life of Our Lord.

Other fragments are located at Astbury, Bowdon, Bromborough, Chester .St. John Baptist, Frodsham, Hilbre, Lyme Park, Macclesfield (West Park), Neston, Over, Overchurch, Prestbury, Wallasey, West Kirby, Wincle (Clulow) and Woodchurch. At most of these places the relics are preserved in churches (for instance Chester St. John Baptist, Neston). One or two crosses have been re-assembled and stand in churchyards (such as Bromborough and Prestbury); while one or two others have been placed in museums (West Kirby and the Grosvenor Museum at Chester).

The fragments generally conform to two main types: In Wirral and Chester are crosses dating from C10 and C11 which combine Anglian, Scandinavian and Irish (Celtic) features. Their shafts are squat-like and highly decorated often with interlace. Also, they possess wheel-shaped crosses with a characteristic ring round each cross. A good collection of such crosses may be seen at Chester St. John Baptist.

The second group of fragments includes crosses in east Cheshire. Usually described as late Mercian (first half of C11), they tended to be set up in pairs as wayside or boundary crosses. In its complete form, each cross consisted of a plain round shaft, at the top of which was a decorated collar. Above the latter was a square section carrying the actual cross. The Macclesfield crosses afford good examples of this type.

Sandbach market square, Anglo-Saxon crosses, late C8/early C9.

Norman (1066 to c.1180)

The Norman style of architecture, like the preceding Anglo-Saxon, was inherited from the Classical styles of ancient Greece and Rome. It was employed in England during the period 1066 to c.1180, but in Cheshire probably not much before 1100. Norman architecture in the county is characterised by the use of masonry of heavy and often dark appearance, this masonry comprising, especially early on, small stones set in thick layers of plaster. There are large round and unmoulded piers, columns and shafts. Above the piers are semi-circular arches which may be single- or sometimes double-stepped. Semi-circular arches are also employed in stone vaulting which occasionally survives locally from the period, as well as on doorways and window-heads. The capitals above piers, columns and shafts tend to be of two main kind: The cushion capital inherited by the Normans from their Anglo-Saxon predecessors, is sometimes plain. Alternatively, it may be decorated with carving of scallops, faces, etc. The other kind of capital is the volute capital which may have originated in Normandy. It is hollow (i.e. concave shaped) with primitive sprigs of foliage on the corners. The most favoured mouldings in Cheshire used on arches and pier capitals are the chevron or zig-zag, and scallop or cone. Occasionally, the cable, billet and nailhead are used as embellishments.

The quantity of Norman work surviving in Cheshire is not great, probably not as much as in other counties of comparable geographical size. Domesday Book (1086) names three churches in Chester (i.e. St. Werburgh's abbey — now the cathedral, Chester St. John Baptist and Chester St. Peter) and nine other churches (Bowdon, Davenham, Frodsham, Legh, Lymm, Northenden, Sandbach, Thornton-le-Moors and Weaverham). It also gives fourteen other parishes which had priests (Acton, Barthomley, Bunbury, Burton [near Tarvin], Eastham, Farndon, Great Budworth, Halton [probably Runcorn], Landican [probably Woodchurch], Neston, Newbould [i.e. Astbury], Newton [i.e. Middlewich], Poulton Lancelyn and Wybunbury). However there is no way of knowing whether the latter group of parishes had churches before the Domesday return was made. Of the twelve churches identified above, only the cathedral, Chester St. John Baptist and Frodsham possess Norman work today, and nearly all of this — if not all — was constructed long after 1086. In addition, there are a few loose stones at Bowdon of Norman origin which may be a trace of the Domesday church.

This brings us to a main consideration, namely that hardly any extant Norman fabric can be positively dated as being earlier than c.1100, and indeed most was erected during the middle or later part of C12. Much of the fabric is primitive and crude, with quite a lot of the latter built rather late in the century. The oldest masonry is at Chester St. John Baptist where the massive piers of the nave arcade were erected immediately before 1100, and at the cathedral in the east wall of the north transept (c.1100). This wall contains a large stepped semi-circular archway and triforium overhead, both characteristically unrefined. Probably the latest and most handsome example of Norman work in Cheshire, dating from c.1180, is the well-moulded doorway at Norton priory, a rare instance of a standard of Norman architecture more common outside the county than in it.

Of surviving Norman work in Cheshire, the most important belongs to the cathedral and its environs. Apart from the gaunt looking north west tower and the north transept, Norman fabric includes the north wall of the north aisle which backs the south side of the cloister. Of English cathedrals based on monastic houses, Chester retains more of its domestic buildings than possibly any other. Work, all belonging to C12, includes the vaulted abbot's chapel (now St. Anselm's chapel), the vaulted undercroft and sections of the cloister. Of particular interest is a doorway on the north side of the cloister with a cusped arch and stiff-leaf foliage (c.1190), a good example of transitional Norman/Early English work.

Next to the cathedral, the most important building — though badly mauled over the centuries — is St. John Baptist in Chester. Of cruciform plan and designed on the grand scale, this church was commenced immediately before the end of C11. After the massive round plain piers of the nave had been erected, the interstitium was constructed followed by the choir, transepts and some of the now-ruined eastern chapels, all taking the major part of C12 to complete. The Norman campaign for building this church originally intended to serve as a cathedral was ended with construction of the triforium (c.1190) with pointed arches, clustered shafts, annulets and finely carved capitals, all displaying transitional Norman/Early English characteristics. Sadly today, much of the original Norman fabric is demolished or in ruins. But hidden inside a Victorian exterior, enough survives to illustrate the grandeur of the Norman intention.

Birkenhead Priory was founded in 1150. Still standing and now serving as a small church for public worship is the chapter-house

Chester St. John Baptist nave, north arcade, late C11/early C12.

Shocklach, St. Edith of Polesworth.

dating from this time. Its main architectural feature is its ribbed quadripartite stone vault.

Three small churches with substantial Norman fabric remain in Cheshire. These all date from mid C12 or slightly later. Two of them, at Shocklach and Bruera, are located near each other in the Dee valley. The third, Prestbury in the east of the county, now serves as a detached chapel sharing the churchyard with the church that replaced it. The walls of Shocklach and Bruera contain the characteristic Norman assembly of small square stones separated by wide mortar joints. Shocklach's south doorway has a thick hoodmould and arch of two orders with mouldings including the cable and chevron. Bruera's main focus of interest is the three-ordered chancel arch. Prestbury chapel which dates from late C12, possesses some of the most refined work in the county, namely an elaborately carved west doorway and tympanum, above which is a unique panel containing seven carved figures.

Sections of Norman work exist in several other churches. Three — Bebington, Frodsham and Middlewich — were clearly important religious centres in C12, being given arcades. Bebington has one aisle, and the two westerly bays of its arcade dividing it from the nave have survived. Middlewich was double-aisled, and it now retains at the east end of the nave the two responds and the two corresponding piers of the arcades. These piers have been reset, possibly in C14, three and a half feet away from the responds with small acutely pointed arches of C14 in between. Frodsham had the most elaborate Norman plan of the three with two aisles, two arcades and a clerestory, of which the Norman arcades and clerestory survive. The arcade piers of each church are plain and round; while above, the arches are stepped. Bebington has capitals decorated with cones divided by reeds, dating from c.1150; Frodsham has capitals with curly volutes and acanthus-leaf decorations; while the capitals of Middlewich display palm leaves and berries. The Norman work in these last two churches dates from c.1170. At another church, Grappenhall, a fragment of C12 masonry survives in the walling over the south arcade in the form of a Norman corbel-table.

In five other churches there are C12 doorways. That at Shotwick of three orders, is retained inside the original Norman south wall of the nave. At Barthomley there is a blocked doorway set in masonry of recent date; and at Church Lawton the main doorway was retained on the south side when the whole of the nave was rebuilt in 1803. There is a small doorway at Stoak, now blocked,

Mellor, Norman font, early C12.

which has a plain semi-circular arch. The Norman north wall at Woodchurch was reconstructed in 1964-65 further to the north of the existing building to accommodate a new north aisle, and a doorway with plain semi-circular arch was moved at the same time to give access to the vestry. Also, the core of the chancel of this church is late C12, possessing in its north wall a single-light splayed window with transitional Norman/Early English features.

There are Norman fonts at Acton, Bebington, Eastham, Grappenhall, Mellor and Mottram-in-Longdendale. Another which used to be at Wallasey is now at Poulton. Of these fonts all of which belong to C12, the finest are at Mellor and Acton.

Several churches possess carved Norman stones, viz. Acton, Bowdon, Bunbury and Burton. At Runcorn, there is a C12 grave slab.

In C18 and C19 known Norman work, mainly of C12 date, was obliterated in nine churches. The following list names these churches together with the identity of the sections destroyed and the dates of destruction:—

Burton — one or possibly two arcades (1721)

Wallasey — a priest's doorway, stoup and tympanum (1760)

Overchurch — a doorway with chevron and pellet ornament (1813)

Thurstaston — a doorway and apse (1824)

Bromborough — whole church consisting of nave and chancel including two south doorways (1828)

Handley — one north doorway (1854)

Ince — one south doorway (1854)

West Kirby — respond with capital and base at west end of nave (1869-70)

Neston — two arcades, each of four arches (1874)

Early English (c.1180 to c.1290)

The Early English style was the first of three Gothic architectural modes to be employed in England. Replacing the Norman, it was used during the period c.1180 to c.1290. The style which is much more sensitive and delicate than Norman architecture, was characterised by the appearance of the acutely pointed arch seen to good effect in lancet windows (themselves typical of the period, but uncommon in Cheshire), arcades, vaulting and doorways. Columns which were frequently detached, became slender though often remaining circular. Capitals were embellished with stiff-leaf foliage, and pedestals were carved with water-holding mouldings. Decorative motifs included the nailhead and dogtooth patterns, examples of both of which occur in the county, though not often.

Of the medieval styles of architecture employed since the Conquest, Early English is the least represented in the county at the present time, less so than even the Norman. Whether this is due to a paucity of building work in C13 or because a number of whole churches, and major portions of churches, known to have possessed Early English fabric were destroyed by C19 "restorers" is not certain. The lost work included (with dates of its destruction:—

Coddington — whole building (1833)

Runcorn — north side of nave and north aisle (1849)

Barthomley — chancel (1852)

Bidston — chancel, nave and aisles (1856)

Dodleston — chancel (1869)

Daresbury — north side of nave (1871)

Eastham — chancel (1863)

The cathedral has Early English work of high quality though some of it is spoilt as a result of over keen restoration. Thus the lady chapel has received much Victorian treatment externally; but internally, most of the walling and all of the triple-shafted vaulting which dates from the second half of C13, retains its Early English purity of design. Possibly the most interesting architectural feature of the cathedral is the early C13 vestibule forming the entrance to the chapter-house, its slender columns devoid of capitals supporting the vaulting. The superb chapter-house (c.1240) is rectangular with lancet windows arranged in even triples and with double arcading. Other Early English sections of the cathedral include a former chapel (now sacristry) to the east of the north transept, the warming room (now song school), the day stairs and the slype.

The Early English style is represented in two other Chester churches. At St. John Baptist the nave clerestory was constructed in C13 when Early English work was at its most mature, the capitals displaying rich foliage. St. Mary de Castro, the small chapel of Chester castle, was built early in C13. The slender shafts and mouldings of the voluted and floriated capitals, as well as the filleted triple-rolls of the vault-ribs, contribute towards making the chapel a delightful surprise and one of the best pieces of the style in Cheshire.

Three major parish churches possess substantial work of the period. They are Acton, Prestbury and Holt. At Acton the whole of the lower part of the embraced tower — complete with lancet windows, archways and pilaster-buttresses — are Early English, as are the piers of the two arcades of the nave. The ornamental motif prevalent in this church is dogtooth moulding but it is not abundant. At Prestbury the nave and chancel come within the period, there being small touches of nailhead moulding and stiff-leaf foliage in the arcades. The chancel of this church possesses — a rarity for Cheshire — a three-light window with lancet tops, the lights being divided by triple-shafted mullions. As for the third church Holt, its whole nave including two arcades of c.1250, is constructed in a version of the style, i.e. octagonal piers and capitals with double-chamfered arches.

Acton, remodelled Early English interior to east, C13.

Other churches retain smaller portions of Early English work. Rostherne has a north nave arcade which is simple in design with round piers and water-holding pedestals. The two arcades at Eastham belong to late C13, the north ornamented with a little nailhead being slightly older than the one on the opposite side of the church. At Wilmslow there is a crypt below the east end of the chancel, the east side of this crypt dating from c.1220.

Three churches display traces of Early English work. The internal shafting of the west doorway of the nave at Nantwich belongs to the period, and was recognised as such by Sir G. Gilbert Scott in mid C19 when he restored the outside of the doorway in a neo-Early English style. At Macclesfield St. Michael the west responds of the two Early English former arcades of the original nave remain *in situ* on either side of the tower archway. The inner doorway giving access to the south aisle of Audlem has on one of its two capitals a stiff-leaf wreath of C13 date. At Sandbach, there are six sculptured heads believed to date from C13.

In several churches there are acutely pointed windows which have uncusped Y-tracery dividing two lights, or intersecting tracery dividing three or more lights. These herald the change of style (c.1290) from Early English to the Decorated, and may therefore be termed transitional Early English/Decorated. One example is the north chancel chapel at Astbury where there are two such windows; another is the south aisle at Bebington with two windows. At Backford the whole of the chancel which has a three-light and a two-light window may be ascribed to this period as can the north chancel chapel at Burton with a single three-light window. The five-light window at the east end of the chancel at Mobberley, if not a Victorian replacement, is also transitional.

There are a small number of stoneware objects, mostly dating from the latter part of C13. Examples include a piscina and aumbry at Backford, and a sedilia and piscina at Mobberley. However, there is only one Early English font and this is at Prestbury. Its value is minimal as it was disastrously recut and refaced in 1857. In the cathedral refectory is a well-preserved stone reading pulpit (c.1290).

Cheshire churches retain little monumental masonry of the period save for some coffin-lids decorated with foliated or floriated crosses. Such objects are found at Bunbury, Burton, Chester St. John Baptist, Dodleston, Nantwich, Tilston, and Witton. There are also several of them in the cloister at the cathedral, including among their number some with intricate and beautiful crosses. At

Burton east end, the window of the north chancel chapel (and if not a rebuild, the chancel window too) displaying Early English/Decorated intersecting tracery, c.1290 to c.1300.

Woodchurch is a C13 wheel-cross. There are three effigies of knights which have lost their original table-tombs. They are at Chester St. John Baptist (said to be a crusader who died in 1192), Grappenhall (1275) and Rostherne (of uncertain C13 date).

Decorated (c.1290 to c.1390)

The second Gothic or Decorated style superseded the Early English about 1290 and lasted till c.1390 in Cheshire, though not as late as this in other parts of the country. Its main characteristics were that arches became less acute and windows were filled with intricate patterns of cusped tracery in their heads. These patterns tended at first to be intersecting or geometrical, then reticulated, and finally flowing. In lesser churches pier capitals and pedestals tended, especially in Cheshire, to be octagonal with double-chamfered mouldings on the arches; but in the greater churches the mouldings were likely to be complex with use of the hollow chamfer, wave, and most of all, the ogee or double-reversed curve. Ornamental foliage on capitals, bosses, etc. — rarely seen in the

Nantwich, Decorated interior to east, C14.

county — became naturalistic. The ballflower though often employed as a Decorated motif elsewhere (e.g. Shropshire) only appears in Cheshire at Birkenhead Priory.

The Decorated style is considerably more in evidence in the county than the earlier styles of architecture, and it is possible to identify a large number of churches with extant Decorated material. However, owing to the frequent overlay of later Perpendicular material, this work is not always evident, especially when observing churches from their exteriors. With the exception of a small number of greater churches whose patrons had access in the first half of C14 to experienced and knowledgeable master-masons, the earlier Decorated work is not very different from the Early English work that preceded it in terms of quality and originality. However as the century advanced, no doubt chiefly due to the Vale Royal influences, the quality of work (for instance at Acton, Bunbury or Nantwich) achieved a degree of sophistication that promised well for C15.

There are two churches which are noteworthy for retaining their Decorated fabric: the cathedral and Nantwich. The latter church with its richly ornamented interior and crumbling exterior stands in a class of its own as a Decorated parish church in Cheshire and, indeed, in the north of England, with the possible exception of Patrington in east Yorkshire. Important as the cathedral's Decorated work is, the accolade of beauty must be awarded to Nantwich, the latter being started and largely completed within a span of one hundred years. Construction commenced at the west end c.1300, and continued progressively towards the east of the building throughout the ensuing century apart from a break of perhaps ten years after the Black Death of 1349. Leaving aside relatively minor work carried out in C15, the church conforms to a mature Decorated style especially in the interstitium and chancel, displaying in its windowing an evolutionary progression in tracery design from the cusped intersecting (in the nave) to the reticulated (in the north transept) and, finally, to the flowing form (in the chancel).

At the start of C14 a big programme of reconstruction was launched at the cathedral. This was begun in the choir where an early Decorated style was utilised, employing some Early English features, such as fillets on the shafting. The unusually large south transept of five bays together with the interstitium came next (c.1340). This Decorated campaign concluded with the building of the south side of the nave and the south aisle (c.1360). All this fabric is extant as well as some other early Decorated reconstructional work carried out (c.1290) in the refectory.

What Decorated work is there elsewhere in the county? Apart from the cathedral and Nantwich (and some timber-framed buildings which may also date from C14 and which will be referred to later), altogether there are some forty churches that still possess fabric of C14 date, most of these buildings being remodelled versions of churches of even older date. In turn, these Decorated churches were almost all remodelled in the Perpendicular style a century later. However, three of the forty like Nantwich, were substantially left unchanged at the end of C14, these being the two-aisled churches of Shotwick and Thornton-le-Moors, and the formerly two-aisled church of Woodchurch.

Of the great number of buildings that received this C15 Perpendicular remodelling, most retained their C14 ground-plan and some, considerable portions of their Decorated fabric. The ground-plan tended to include a broad nave, two aisles with sometimes the north narrower than the south, low arcades, steep gabled roofs without parapets, a three-bay chancel devoid of chancel chapels, narrow cusped two-light side windows and a west tower. There is no record of any clerestory being included in this plan in Cheshire. Relying on evidence provided by surviving Decorated work, it is possible to identify the following churches which have kept their C14 ground-plans: Astbury, Audlem, Bunbury, Chester St. Mary, Great Budworth, Malpas, Middlewich, Mobberley, Nether Alderley, Pott Shrigley, Tarvin, Waverton, West Kirby, Wilmslow and Witton.

Within the group of forty churches, those which retain considerable portions of their Decorated fabric include:—

Astbury — tower (with parapet spire); aisles; south chancel chapel; two porches

Audlem — tower; chancel; north aisle; north chancel chapel

Bunbury — tower; chancel; treasury; parts of south aisle and south porch

Great Budworth — north aisle; north aisle chapel; parts of nave and chancel

Malpas — tower; crypt; parts of chancel and aisles

Middlewich — parts of tower, nave and chancel

Mobberley — parts of nave, chancel and aisles

Tarvin — south aisle; part of nave

West Kirby — north chancel chapel; parts of chancel and north aisle

Wilmslow — parts of nave and aisles

Woodchurch — tower; parts of nave, south aisle and chancel

To this group may be added Frodsham, a C14 rebuild of a Norman church (Decorated tower and north aisle; and part of chancel).

Another sub-group of the forty churches have isolated but substantial C14 portions which are largely unspoilt by subsequent alterations. These portions are:—

Towers Bebington (with broach spire), Chester St. Peter, Eastham (with broach spire re-assembled in 1751), Holt

Nave arcades Chester St. Michael (1), Pott Shrigley (1), Tarporley (2, including one with rare hexagonal piers), Waverton (2), Witton (2)

Chancels	Ince, Shocklach, Stockport St. Mary
Aisles	Rostherne and Prestbury (1 each)
Chapels	Acton, Grappenhall, Rostherne, Stockport St. Mary (1 each)
Porch	Bebington
Miscellaneous	Birkenhead (scriptorium), Chester St. Mary de Castro (crypt).

Another sub-group possess now-solitary Decorated features which were preserved or re-used when the buildings were later reconstructed. The chief examples are:—

Acton	— chancel arch
Chester St. Mary	— tower arch and chancel arch
Great Budworth	— tower arch
Tarvin	— tower arch
Witton	— chancel arch (now part of north arcade), tower arch.

Also in this sub-group may be included several portions of towers, only the Decorated lower sections remaining. These are Congleton (encased in masonry in C18), Farndon, Heswall (a late C14 instance), Middlewich and Neston. Some of these towers were heightened in C15 or C16 (e.g. Middlewich, Heswall) possibly in anticipation of a nave clerestory which may or may not have been built.

Special mention should be made of Acton. Here the body of the church was remodelled partly at the end of C14 and partly at the beginning of C15 as a continuous follow-on. The building displays features which may be interpreted as transitional between the Decorated and Perpendicular styles. For example, the side windows of the south aisle and of the chancel contain tracery mullions illustrating this changeover.

A feature of the Decorated work in Cheshire during C14 is the almost total use of large blocks of ashlar hewn from local quarries of sandstone. When further reconstruction took place in subsequent centuries, the general practice was for this material to be carefully dismantled and re-assembled.

In the county practically every kind of Decorated tracery is found in C14 windows. For instance at Nantwich early C14 cusped intersecting tracery appears in seven aisle windows. Geometrical tracery is rare but can be seen in the east window of the north aisle at Malpas. Reticulated tracery, however, is common as at Bunbury in the great west window of the tower or at West Kirby in the chancel east window (the latter renewed in C19). Flowing tracery is fairly uncommon, but is featured for instance in the east windows of the chancels at Thornton-le-Moors and Bunbury. Also, the side windows of the chancel at Nantwich display flowing tracery complete with sacred hearts. An interesting variant of flowing tracery is found in the chancel east window at Audlem which displays distinct transitional Decorated/Perpendicular characteristics (c.1400).

Decorated window-arches have inherited their two-centred shape from the Early English lancet design. They are all sharply pointed (for example at Nantwich or Bunbury in their chancels). In a few churches (as at Acton, Grappenhall and Tarvin), there are Decorated windows with square heads.

Though the plain chamfer was still used for mouldings on arches, window-frames and doorways, the wave-moulding was introduced early in C14 as was the ogee and hollow chamfer. The wave-moulding often appears in pairs with one wave larger than the other, as on the chancel arch at Acton. Where two mouldings — not necessarily of the same kind — appear side by side, they tend to be separated by a simple quirk, later by a cavetto, and occasionally by a step. The double-ogee, usually mirrored, also became popular during the period. In Cheshire, all these mouldings were used throughout C15 and C16 too. They cannot, therefore, be taken on their own as evidence of C14 Decorated work.

Fifteen churches including the cathedral contain between them twenty two Decorated nave arcades. In the lesser churches especially, piers and capitals (and bases too) tend to be octagonal in form. Thus of the twenty two arcades, fourteen have octagonal piers, with octagonal capitals in nearly every case. Instances include Middlewich, Thornton-le-Moors and Woodchurch. Churches with sets of piers and capitals which have dispensed with the simple octagonal form are mainly the greater churches. This group comprises the cathedral (south arcade), Great Budworth (north arcade), Nantwich (both arcades), Pott Shrigley (north arcade), Tarporley (south arcade) and Witton (both arcades). In the piers of most of these six churches, three quarter round

Bunbury chancel, Decorated east window with flowing tracery, late C14.

shafts are placed on the cardinal sides with a variety of patterns for the diagonals, ranging from half-round shafts at the cathedral to flat chamfers at Nantwich and hollows at Great Budworth and Witton. Pott Shrigley with its two-bay nave possesses one trefoiled pier with three half-round shafts; while Tarporley has plain hexagonal piers. In the earlier capitals (for instance Eastham, Mobberley or Nantwich) and sometimes in the bases (such as Nantwich), the bell form appears. It is unusual in Cheshire churches for floral or other highly ornamental designs to be included on capitals. Examples of such embellishments include fleurons at Chester St. Michael and Middlewich, and more intricate floral carving on the interstitium capitals at Nantwich.

When C15/C16 reconstruction took place, stronger external support was called for in the form of new deeper Perpendicular buttressing. For this reason, earlier Decorated buttresses are few in Cheshire. The simplest and probably earliest buttresses had one or two offsets only, with a short sloping head (such as Astbury south side, or Thornton-le-Moors). Several large churches (for instance Bunbury chancel or Nantwich nave) have well developed and suitably proportioned buttresses with gabled and sloping heads. The most elaborate buttresses of all support the transepts and chancel at Nantwich. Plain for half their height, they then step back. From this level upwards, the buttresses are enriched with shafting, panelling and blind tracery, pinnacles, gables and crocketed spirelets.

Stoneware: In the lady chapel of the cathedral is the re-assembled shrine of St. Werburgh. A small number of churches have sedilia. Good examples are at Acton, Bunbury, Malpas (two sets), Nantwich and Stockport St. Mary. Those at the latter two churches are elaborate with projecting canopies and rich displays of carving. Piscinas of the period are more common than sedilia, being combined with sedilia where the latter are present, or located on their own especially in side-chapels as in the south chancel chapel at Astbury. At Nantwich there is a rare Easter sepulchre on the north side of the sanctuary, and at Stockport St. Mary another. Reredoses: Two only remain, these at Bunbury and Witton. Fonts are also few, the better of two at Nether Alderley. This last font has a plain circular bowl supported by four heads and foliage; the other at Shotwick has a plain octagonal bowl only.

Tombs and memorials: The period is represented mainly by effigies of knights which have lost their tombs, the result of maltreatment. The list includes Bowdon (two, c.1320 and 1340), Bunbury (of uncertain C14 or even C15 date), Chester St. John

Baptist (a lady of c.1347, and a priest of C14 date), Farndon (c.1340), Marton (two of uncertain C14 date) and Nantwich (c.1390). A small number of effigied table-tombs or effigies in canopied recesses have survived as well, and some of them are in quite good condition, viz. Acton (1399), Astbury (c.1371), Barthomley (c.1390), Bunbury (1394) and Stockport St. Mary (1334). With the exception of the tomb at Stockport which possesses the effigy of a priest, the other effigied tombs are all of knights.

In the churchyard of Astbury are four effigies of uncertain C14 date, of which two (a knight and lady) are displayed under a red sandstone canopy. The other two (a knight and a priest) lie in the open, weathered to two blocks of stone. There is only one effigy-less table-tomb of the period in the county and this (c.1300) is at Chester cathedral. The remaining C14 items include a small white alabaster plaque at Heswall, a stone slab with small metal plaque (removed elsewhere in the church) at Malpas, and a stone slab with a floriated cross at Neston, all three of indeterminate C14 date.

Stained glass: There is little C14 stained glass in the county and none older than this period. What there is, apart from fragments in other churches, is located in three buildings: At Tattenhall are

Astbury churchyard, group of Decorated tombs, C14.

displayed in the chancel two saints including St. Alban the patron saint of the church. At Grappenhall in the south chancel chapel are the figures of seven saints all of which bar one can be identified by means of emblems or scrolls written in Lombardic capitals. At Shotwick the east window of the north aisle contains two figures forming an Annunciation group. This last glass is believed to be the only C14 glass in the county which remains in its original setting.

Timberwork: Apart from timber-framed buildings, there is little timberwork left in Cheshire. Of that which survives, the best by far are the spiky canopied choir-stalls of late C14 date at Chester cathedral and at Nantwich, both sets being probably the most beautiful and intricate of their period in the country. In two churches, Stockport St. Mary (chancel) and Tarvin (south aisle), there are single-framed roofs; while in the second of these buildings is a well preserved Decorated screen constructed in the style of imitation open stonework. Lastly but not least, there is an early C14 timber pulpit at Mellor believed to be the oldest in England.

Cheshire is known to have lost some Decorated work in C19, the result of over-restoration of some of its churches. The list of destroyed C14 work includes:—

Stockport St. Mary	—	south aisle and west window (1812)
Davenham	—	whole building (1844-1870)
Runcorn	—	tower (1849)
Lymm	—	chancel arch (1851)
Aldford	—	tower and spire (1866)
Tarporley	—	chancel, south aisle and south porch (1869)
Grappenhall	—	south aisle (1874)

Perpendicular (c.1390 to 1558)

The final phase of Gothic architecture was a long one. Elsewhere in England it started about the time of the Black Death, but there is no evidence that it came to Cheshire before c.1400. It lasted in full vigour in the county until the Suppression (1540) before tailing to an insignificant level by the commencement of the reign of Elizabeth I in 1558. Sometimes the variant of Perpendicular used after 1485 is known as Tudor.

Mellor, Decorated pulpit, C14.

Alternatively called "rectilinear", Perpendicular was the only style of architecture native to England. Characterised by an emphasis on height, verticality and parallel lines, it represented a puritanical reaction against the curvilinear excesses of the Decorated period. Its main features were big and high windows occupying a maximum of wall-space. The windows were divided many times by mullions running vertically upwards to their heads and by transoms, permitting large areas of stained glass panelling to be inserted.

The style was marked by the emergence of the four-centred obtusely pointed arch in arcades, vaulting, doorways and window-heads. Towards the end of C15, the four-centred arch evolved into the particularly flattened and graceful version known as the Tudor arch frequently set under a label or square surround. Arcades became taller and their piers slenderer. Roofs earlier supplied with lierne-vaulting, changed during the period to having star-vaulting and — probably the most characteristic roof design of the period — to fan-traceried vaulting. On piers the casement moulding was commonly used in conjunction with slender composite shafting. When capitals were employed, they consisted of the nominal small or "plant-pot" type. Motifs were the quatrefoil, Tudor rose and portcullis often employed in combination with recessed and ribbed panelling on walls.

The Perpendicular period in Cheshire was a time of considerable activity in the reconstruction of churches, a period which continued vigorously until the Suppression. The surviving fabric, especially in the west of the county where C19 church restorers left much of it in its original condition, conforms to a high standard of design and workmanship in which a genuine vernacular style is detectable and which was employed both in the latter part of C15 and in the first half of C16. Ornamentally, the stonework never reaches the complexity of design found in some other areas of the country, but it does make the maximum use of the available sandstone — as in the construction of the towers at Tarvin or Wybunbury, or the nave and aisles at Malpas. Craftsmanship in the county during the period reached its highest levels of perfection in the products of the stained glass designers — work now nearly all perished — and in the outputs of the woodcarvers and carpenters. Fortunately much of the labours of these last two groups does survive in the roofs and screens of many churches, and the timber they employed does overcome the disadvantages of having to construct with stone prone to rapid weathering.

The extent to which the Perpendicular style has completely dominated church building in Cheshire, can be demonstrated with a few statistical facts. The small population of the county at the time of Domesday, gradually increased during the later medieval period (after the Black Death in the intervening period had reduced the populace by one third). This increase was matched by the establishment of many additional churches to meet the spiritual needs of the people. By 1558 there were probably 131 churches available for public worship in the county. Of these, eighty nine buildings survive with material that was constructed before 1558. And of these eighty nine churches, as many as sixty eight have C15/C16 Perpendicular work represented in their fabric.

The sixty eight Perpendicular churches may be classed as follows:—

1. There is a group of nine churches, the fabric of which substantially dates from C15/C16. This is not to say that in every case they were first built in the period after c.1400, simply that no earlier material has survived. The group includes Brereton, Cheadle, Gawsworth, Marbury, Plemstall, Sandbach, Tilston, Weaverham and Wrenbury. In addition Disley might deserve to be assigned to this category were it not for the fact that much of its so-called Perpendicular fabric was reconstructed in early C19. Gawsworth occupies a rare chronological niche for churches in Cheshire in that its nave was commenced relatively early in C15 (i.e. c.1430) when little building in stone appeared to be taking place elsewhere in the county. All the other churches of the group were started during the last quarter of the same century or during the first half of C16.

2. A group of twenty five churches were extensively remodelled in Perpendicular times but which can be identified as having retained an earlier ground-plan. These are Astbury (C14 ground-plan), Audlem (C14), Barthomley (C13?), Bunbury (C14), Chester St. Mary (C14), Chester St. Peter (C14?), Eastham (C13), Grappenhall (C12?), Great Budworth (C14), Holt (C13), Malpas (C14), Middlewich (C14), Mobberley (C14), Mottram-in-Longdendale (C14?), Nether Alderley (C14), Pott Shrigley (C14), Prestbury (C13), Rostherne (C13), Tarporley (C14), Tarvin (C14), Tattenhall (C14?), Waverton (C14), Wilmslow (C14), Over (C14?) and Witton (C14). As the question marks show, there is uncertainty over the dating of the ground-plans of some of these buildings.

3. Ten churches comprise a group which have largely kept their earlier fabric, but to which Perpendicular work has been added without the need for wholesale remodelling. The churches (with the Perpendicular work indicated in brackets) are Acton (part of chancel including the east window), Bebington (the whole east end of the building), Bruera (south nave chapel), the cathedral (part of nave, north aisle, part of transepts, south porch), Frodsham (part of chancel, north chancel chapel), Nantwich (nave clerestory, east window of chancel, part of south transept, south porch), Shotwick (tower), Thornton-le-Moors (part of tower, south chancel chapel), West Kirby (tower, part of north aisle) and Woodchurch (south porch). None of this Perpendicular work with the exception of the window at the east end of the chancel and the windows of the south transept of Nantwich, is early. The chancel east window of this last church which is markedly subarcuated, is transitional Decorated/Perpendicular with a leaning, if any, towards the later style. The great window at the south end of the south transept — arguably the finest Perpendicular window in the county — was inserted slightly later than the chancel window and represents a true early style which may have come to Cheshire from Lichfield.
4. The final group within the sixty eight churches comprises twenty four buildings which have been largely rebuilt during the last three hundred years but which retain a minor amount of Perpendicular work, usually the tower. Examples include Handley (tower), Taxal (tower) and Upper Peover (south nave chapel).

As mentioned earlier, the Perpendicular style came quite late to Cheshire where it developed a number of characteristics giving it a flavour of its own. These distinctive features when looked at separately, are not all confined to Cheshire. They are as follows:—

a. *Transoms* were placed high across windows at their shoulders (with good examples at Barthomley, Bunbury and Malpas). It has been suggested that this tracery was set high in the arch to reduce erosion.
b. *Window-arches* tended to be elliptical (as at Barthomley) or segmental (for instance Tarvin).
c. *Cusping* As time passed in the later medieval period, window-cusps became less pronounced (as at Malpas), then partially eliminated (as at Bebington), and finally completely eliminated (for instance in the Ridley chapel at Bunbury).

d. *Buttresses* These became very deep, dividing closely set but broad aisle windows (such as Bunbury or Holt).

e. *Clerestories* The tendency was for windows to be set increasingly close together (such as Brereton or Barthomley).

f. *Embattled parapets* had mouldings that were continuous, not only along the tops of the merlons and embrasures, but down their sides too (for instance Great Budworth or Malpas).

g. *Tower friezes* Often there appeared a frieze displaying quatrefoils or saltires below the parapet (as at Middlewich, Over and Weaverham).

h. *Roofs* Camber-beam roofs were ornamented with many bosses and crows' feet (for example Disley, Witton).

Towers: There are forty six towers which retain a substantial amount of Perpendicular masonry, all this work being constructed in late C15, or early or mid C16. What have these towers got in common? Probably not a lot. They are nearly all constructed of large blocks of sandstone and few of them exceed sixty feet in height. Apart from a few (such as Tarvin or

Brereton nave, part of Perpendicular clerestory, late C15/early C16.

Wybunbury), they display little external decoration and many have lost their original pinnacles. However, several groups of towers do possess features in common which are readily observable. These are:—

1. *Macclesfield St. Michael, Tarvin and Wybunbury* Among the most handsome of Cheshire towers, this group possess clasped buttresses, a double-windowed belfry and a frieze below the parapet.

2. *Barthomley, Middlewich and Sandbach* The belfries of these towers have on each side two windows under a common hoodmould or canopy. Immediately above this canopy and below the parapet is a frieze. The buttresses are diagonal.

3. *Shotwick, Backford, Handley and Tattenhall* These small three-stage towers were all built c.1500 by the same gang of masons. They all have single three-light belfry windows with hoodmoulds as well as diagonal buttresses, eight pinnacles (if not lost), internal vices and Tudor west doorways.

4. *Great Budworth and Witton* Both these large towers were assembled by Thomas Hunter in early C16. Their chief common characteristic is in having double windows with separate hoodmoulds, lighting their belfries.

5. *Mobberley and Nether Alderley* Richard Platt constructed both towers c.1533. Of four stages, they are of the two-window type. Also they have diagonal buttresses and internal vices. They used to have eight pinnacles but these have now disappeared.

6. *Daresbury and Grappenhall* Of similar general proportions these plain towers have belfry windows which are single, of the two-light type and with hoodmoulds. Also they possess diagonal buttresses and internal vices.

Weaverham is not matched precisely in its main appearance by any other tower in the county. It does, however, have several Cheshire characteristics such as three-light single belfry windows with hoodmoulds, a frieze under the parapet, diagonal buttresses, an internal vice, west doorway and (formerly) eight pinnacles. These, taken with its height and excellent proportions, make it possibly the most representative of all Perpendicular towers in the county.

Nave arcades and clerestories: There are sixteen churches with two Perpendicular arcades surviving, and seven with one. In the majority of cases the octagonal pier with simple octagonal capital continued to be erected in C15 and C16 (as at Audlem and Weaverham). In eight greater churches (Astbury, Barthomley, Bebington [bay 1], Brereton, Bunbury, the cathedral, Great Budworth and Malpas), the piers which are derived from the basic octagonal form, are clustered. The simplest pier pattern consists of half-round shafts on the cardinal sides with plain chamfers (at Barthomley which appears to be a C15 copy of the C14 nave at Nantwich), or hollow chamfers (Brereton and Bunbury) on the diagonals. At Astbury and Great Budworth the half-rounds have been replaced by triple-round shafts; while at the cathedral the diagonal chamfers have been substituted by small half-round shafts. The arrangement is carried a stage further at Malpas where each pier consists of a series of alternating half-rounds and hollows. The most complex pattern of all is at Bebington where there is an asymmetrical arrangement of small triple-shafts, hollows and other mouldings. The capitals above the piers of most of these churches tend to be small, and in one or two cases the hollows run through to the apex of the arch (as at Bunbury). At Astbury the capitals have disappeared completely.

Barthomley, Perpendicular interior to east, late C15.

Nineteen churches have Perpendicular clerestories. Of these churches, five are of the east Cheshire type (Cheadle, Mobberley, Nether Alderley, Prestbury and Wilmslow). Their clerestories give the impression of being long and low, with two-light windows well spaced out and gabled roofs overlapping the walls. The other fourteen belong to the west Cheshire type, all possessing higher clerestories with windows containing a variety of number of lights, under embattled parapets. The intention in constructing these west Cheshire clerestories appears to have been to enlarge the area of the windows at the expense of the walling.

Thus the earliest is at Great Budworth where the windows are rather low below the parapet and are placed between fairly long sections of wall. The intermediate kind where the amount of walling approximately equals the windowing is displayed at Sandbach and Malpas. Next comes Witton where the windows are quite close together. In the final and possibly latest stage, the windows run on one from the previous one. Audlem, Barthomley and Brereton are good examples of this, but the best of all is Astbury where the clerestory windows not only touch each other but occupy the maximum vertical space between the aisle-roofs and the parapet strings, thus providing the maximum "greenhouse" effect.

Chancels: Perpendicular chancels — some original and others which are reconstructed earlier chancels — number twenty. In the case of one or two (for instance Malpas), the task of re-assembly involved little more than taking down and remounting the ashlar walls and in inserting new windows at the sides and at the east end. Sometimes more ambitious schemes were carried out involving the construction of side arcades to give access to chantry or guild chapels (for example Great Budworth, Holt or Middlewich). Even more innovative was the provision of chancel clerestories (e.g. Frodsham). Not infrequently the old chancel arch was hidden in C15 or C16 behind a new rood-screen, and when the rood and often its screen were swept away in Protestant times the older arch was exposed once more (as at Acton).

In some churches, partial reconstruction at the east end called for removal of the chancel arch completely (for example Holt and Witton), a reversion by Perpendicular masons to an earlier plan of church, the "through-church". The most drastic form of rebuilding was to replace the whole chancel often at the same time as the nave (as at Astbury and Plemstall). In such cases the aim was to make the chancel large, airy and light. In one or two churches which had been appropriated to a monastery and where financial responsibility for upkeep and rebuilding of the chancel rested with the abbot or prior, the chancel was not rebuilt (a good example being Audlem), even though the nave and side-aisles the responsibility of the parishioners had been attended to.

Aisles: There are twenty five churches with Perpendicular north aisles and twenty eight with Perpendicular south aisles, and of all of these churches twenty one have both north and south Perpendicular aisles. Since earlier, Decorated churches frequently had wide aisles especially on their south sides, this C15 or C16 reconstruction tended to occupy the same ground-plan where higher walls would be raised accommodating larger windows (for example Bunbury, Malpas and Over). Occasionally the old walls were retained as far as the cills and the new work was erected on top. Instances can clearly be seen at Audlem (south aisle), Bunbury (south aisle) and Malpas (both aisles). As with windows of clerestories and chancels, the general aim was to maximise the spaciousness and light of the aisles. Thus the windows gradually became larger in aisle-walls, the small space between being retained for deep and narrow projecting buttresses. There are many excellent instances in the county of facades of aisles which display such features, i.e. large Perpendicular windows filling each bay and almost touching the buttresses on either side. Above, the windows reach nearly to the deep battlemented parapets; while below, the cills rest over well-formed and heavy base-moulds (for instance Barthomley north aisle, Bebington both aisles, Great Budworth south aisle, Plemstall south side of nave, and Tarvin north aisle).

Chapels: The late medieval period was an age when chantry chapels became increasingly popular and many were founded or refounded in Cheshire churches at that time. Some surviving chapels are located singly to one side of the chancel (e.g. Thornton-le-Moors south side, Bunbury south side) or on both sides of the chancel (for instance Bebington or Tarporley). Occasionally there is a chapel to the north or south of a nave (as at Bruera) or an aisle (e.g. Wilmslow). In Cheshire there are thirty Perpendicular chapels having a distinct structural identity, i.e. are not simply a fenced-off portion of, say, an aisle. Of these chapels, twenty four are north or south chancel chapels, and six are appendages to other portions of church buildings. Owing to the religious upheavals of C16 and C17, not many of the chapels with such a distinct identity remain in their original architectural condition, and indeed nearly all were converted to use as mortuary chapels for the peerage and landed gentry. There are several however which have not been badly maltreated and are worthy of careful examination, notably the south chancel chapels at Barthomley and Bunbury. The architectural features of the majority of these chapels, built in late C15 or early C16, tend to be like those of the aisles and chancels of their churches.

In a number of churches, areas were fenced off by timber screens as chantry chapels in side-aisles especially at the east end. Instances survive at Barthomley (north aisle), and Cheadle and Northenden (both aisles in each of these churches). The identity of many of these chapels, however, has been lost often as a result of the destruction of the screens, but a few are indicated by the presence of a piscina (for example Marbury or Wrenbury).

Porches: Eighteen Perpendicular porches have survived, a smaller number than there were before C18 and C19 when many porches were destroyed by "restorers". Two porches are of three storeys (Astbury and Macclesfield St. Michael), five are of two storeys (the cathedral, Malpas, Middlewich, Nantwich and Over), and the remainder of one storey. Of these eighteen porches, fourteen are on the south side, two on the west and two on the north. The best proportioned of the one storey porches are located at Barthomley, Great Budworth and Witton. This type which is more common in the west of the county than the east and which conforms to the west Cheshire style, is box-like with a horizontal battlement across the front. The porch at Malpas is probably the most handsome of the two-storey type, and it complements the south aisle of the church in a satisfying manner. Both of the three-storey porches have much to commend them, though that at Astbury which rises to the full height of the nave roof retains much of its original masonry, unlike that at Macclesfield.

Windows: In mid C15 window-arches tended to be somewhat acute or two-pointed. Examples of this early Perpendicular feature can be seen at Gawsworth (south side of nave) and Nantwich (south transept). Towards the end of the century, and continuing in C16, the Tudor or four-centred arch came to be used as well as the elliptical and segmental versions of arches already referred to. A church which displays these three kinds is Bunbury (south chancel chapel east window — Tudor; south aisle windows — elliptical; north aisle windows — segmental). The chancel east windows of some churches have Tudor heads, such as Brereton and Frodsham (the latter a magnificent seven-light specimen). Later in C16 window-arches tended to be superseded by square heads (as at Rostherne and Wilmslow).

As time progressed in the Perpendicular period, the number of window-lights increased from an average of two or three in early C15 to four or five in late C15 and early C16, in order to accommodate a greater number of pieces of stained glass. This development is well illustrated at Over where there are four and five light windows along the same wall of the south aisle. Sometimes the three-light pattern was retained in later Perpendicular times, as at Plemstall or Wrenbury.

In all windows constructed in the Perpendicular style, i.e. after c.1400, the mullions rise vertically to the window-arch or square head, and in Cheshire there are no exceptions to this rule. Subarcuated or arched tracery, a trait inherited from the earlier Decorated period, survived in a number of churches in a modified and somewhat artificial form until quite late (for instance Malpas and Bunbury aisles) before disappearing as at Tarvin. Often the tracery in the arch was made to accommodate a large square or rectangular central panel (e.g. Bunbury south chancel chapel east window) or several long panels of approximately equal size (e.g. Tarporley south chancel chapel).

Buttresses: These appear to have followed on in design from C14 Decorated models at Nantwich. Typically, Perpendicular buttresses have a deep projection (as at Acton and Malpas). This type has one offset halfway up, an embellished gable at the top, and behind the latter a section sloping up to the string of the roof parapet. At other churches (such as Bunbury or Tarvin) the type was modified in its proportions, becoming less elegant. Somewhat later, the gable and other decorative work disappeared (as at Tarporley and Bunbury south chancel chapels). In its final or debased form, seen at Waverton and Wrenbury, the Perpendicular buttress became a plain and chunky but still functional block of masonry.

Parapets: It is commonplace for Perpendicular work of all kinds to be crowned with parapets — towers, nave and chancel clerestories, and aisles and roofs. In almost all cases the original parapets — constructed in C15 or C16 — are embattled, an ecclesiastical feature not often found elsewhere in Europe. However in a small number of churches in the county, Perpendicular parapets are straight and plain (for example Bebington chancel, Brereton aisles, and Acton aisles). In those cases where embattled parapets lack continuous mouldings in the Cheshire style, it is safe to assume that they are C19 replacements (e.g. Middlewich, Nantwich) and not originals.

Many Perpendicular parapets carry pinnacles, there being numerous arrays for instance on the roofs at Malpas and Marbury. Many such pinnacles are undoubtedly C19 or C20 replacements. A number of churches carry unsightly stumps especially on towers (e.g. Bidston and Grappenhall, with eight pinnacles missing on each). Frequently the bases of pinnacles rise from panelled shafts which run vertically up the exteriors or angles of parapet faces. Such shafting normally originates at the level of string mouldings at the bottom of parapets, or in the heads of buttresses.

Another characteristic, featured prominently in the county, is for string courses at the bases of parapets to be prominently decorated with fleurons, small animals, grotesques and sometimes small shields. There is an exceptionally good example of this style of embellishment at Tarvin (north aisle). Not infrequently, the carvings are crudely executed (as at Wrenbury), indicating the handiwork of local craftsmen.

Doorways: Perpendicular doorways in Cheshire are nearly all small and are generally restricted to a small number of positions along the walls of church buildings. These positions are the south side of the chancel (for instance the priest's doorway at Brereton and the patron's doorway at Gawsworth), the south side of the south chancel chapel (e.g. Tarporley), both sides of the nave (e.g. Tilston), north and south aisles (e.g. Bunbury), and west side of west towers (of which there are many instances including Bidston, Holmes Chapel and Marbury).

As with arcade arches and window-arches, the Perpendicular arches of doorways are frequently four-centred, those dating from C16 tending to be more flattened or Tudor-shaped (such as the tower west doorways of Barthomley and Handley). But the precise shape of an arch is not necessarily an exact indicator of the age of a doorway. Thus there are some with the two-centred form (such as the west doorways of the towers of Wybunbury and Weaverham) that were built quite late. Some Tudor arches are framed in labels and in such cases the spandrels, head and jambs may be intricately decorated. In particular, the west doorway of the tower at Waverton, the south doorway at Holt and the north doorway at Chester St. Mary deserve inspection. Though not framed in a label, the tower west doorway at Tarvin must be included in this handsome group of embellished Tudor doorways.

Mouldings: Perpendicular base-mouldings which run along external walls below cills of windows often continue round buttresses and porches too. Tending towards a compexity in pattern, these mouldings can be divided into two groups. Approximately two thirds of the way up the outside wall below the cill is a projecting moulding which serves as an eave to throw the rainwater off the vertical wall. Lower down and approximately one third up the wall is a moulded plinth. Typically this double arrangement can be seen at Over (south aisle) where the projecting moulding consists of a reversed ogee terminating in a nosing below. The plinth has a simple chamfered moulding. In some of the greater churches of Cheshire there are three sets of base-mouldings, the third set being another projecting moulding between the other two (as at Tarvin north aisle and Bunbury south chancel chapel).

Perpendicular mouldings round doorways and on inner tower archways vary considerably in design. Often, masons working in C15 and C16 relied on the well-used mouldings of the previous two centuries. Thus the deep hollow or cavetto of C13 appears quite frequently (as on the west doorways of Barthomley and Gawsworth). There is, however, a much greater use of C14 mouldings than C13 ones such as the plain chamfer (as at Grappenhall), the hollow chamfer (e.g. Little Budworth), the wave (e.g. Wybunbury) and the double-ogee (e.g. Barthomley).

Stoneware: Rather surprisingly in view of the large amount of Perpendicular work in the county, there are few instances of stoneware other than fonts and tombs. There is one early Perpendicular pulpit and accompanying remaining half of a chancel screen at Nantwich (both c.1400). Also, there is a C16 screen at Bunbury which, like the Nantwich artefacts, is of high quality. There are a few sedilia and piscinas sometimes combined (as at Acton, Frodsham, Malpas and Middlewich). Of fonts there are at least seventeen which can be attributed to the period. The majority of them possess octagonal bowls with quatrefoiled panels. Good examples may be seen at Astbury, Goostrey, Great Budworth and Malpas. The best of the group which is intricately carved, is at Holt.

Tombs and other memorials: Predictably the Perpendicular period is better represented in memorials for the dead etc. than earlier periods. The extant work which is in better condition generally than the work surviving from C14 and before, is of three kinds: First and most numerous are effigies either supported on table-tombs or placed within canopies which may be recessed in a wall. Two of these memorials are of high quality — the effigies of a knight and his lady in a chancel tomb recess at Macclesfield St. Michael (1495), and the effigies of a knight and his lady lying on a table-tomb at Malpas (1522). Other effigied tombs are to be found at Barthomley (priest on a table-tomb, 1529), Cheadle (two knights on a table-tomb, C15 or C16), Macclesfield St. Michael (knight in a canopied recess, 1492; ditto 1527; knight and his lady in a canopied recess, 1528), Mottram-in-Longdendale (knight and his lady on a low table-tomb, early C15), Upper Peover (knight and his lady in a canopied recess, c.1456; and another knight and his lady on a table-tomb, c.1483), and Wilmslow (priest on a table-tomb, 1537; civilian and his wife in adjacent canopied recesses, 1536).

The second and smaller group of memorials consists of incised slabs, mostly portraying figures of the departed. The list comprises Birkenhead (plain inscription to a cleric, 1473), Malpas (figure of a cleric, 1495), Mottram-in-Longdendale (figure of cleric, 1517), and Prestbury (one with figure of civilian, 1482; and another with figures of knight & lady, 1495).

The third and smallest group of Perpendicular memorials consists of three brasses. These are located at Chester St. Peter (lawyer, c.1460), Macclesfield St. Michael (the famous and unique "Pardon" brass, 1506), and Wilmslow (knight & lady, 1460).

Stained glass: In Cheshire there is as little C15 and C16 stained glass as that belonging to C14. There are a number of fragments re-assembled in at least seven churches such as Mobberley and Upper Peover. Possibly the only church with more than some fragments of Cheshire-made glass is Grappenhall where there is a figure of a female saint. Two churches, Disley and Birtles, do contain fairly large quantities of glass of the period, some of which, particularly at Birtles, is of high quality and colour. Most of this glass of both churches appears to have come from the continent.

Timberwork: Development of the high and thin-walled Perpendicular clerestories led to the installation of camber-beam roofs in many Cheshire churches. These roofs are often supported additionally by wall-posts, and are tied by arch-braces springing from the wall-posts to curve inwards to the camber-beams. The area of the roof is divided into panels, the intersections of which are covered with square or circular bosses. Frequently the latter are made to look even more ornate, being fringed with small decorative objects called crows' feet. The cross-timbers are richly moulded with hollows and rounds, and sometimes the panels and wall-posts are decorated too. The following roofs are among the best: Astbury (nave, chancel and south aisle), Audlem (nave), Barthomley (nave and north aisle), Bowdon (north and south aisles), Chester St. Mary (nave), Disley (nave), Malpas (nave), Mobberley (nave), and Witton (nave and chancel).

Astbury south aisle, roof detail, late C15.

One late C15 timber pulpit survives in the county at Marbury. This is octagonal in shape and rests on a new stone base. At Astbury there is an early C16 wooden lectern. The latter is the only medieval one in the county (save for a foreign one at Birtles).

Cheshire retains a number of late medieval screens and remnants of screens, some of which are of remarkably high quality. Three were originally rood-screens, but having now lost their parapets, serve as chancel screens. The two outstanding instances are at Astbury (c.1500) and Mobberley (dated 1500); a third which is a plainer construction, is at Siddington. Churches with remnants of rood-screens include Daresbury, Plemstall, Shotwick, Stoak and Weaverham. In addition, several buildings retain their Perpendicular parclose screens. These are Astbury (c.1500), Barthomley (early C16), Cheadle (1529), Malpas (1514), Northenden (1527), Plemstall (early C16) and Wilmslow (early C16).

As happened in earlier periods with older styles of architecture, much Perpendicular work was destroyed in C18 and C19. Known instances of destruction include:—

Mobberley, chancel screen, 1500.

Burton	—	tower (1721)
Rostherne	—	tower (1741)
Stockport St. Mary	—	tower, nave (1812)
Disley	—	body of church (1824)
Sandbach	—	tower, south porch (1847)
Lymm	—	nave and aisles (1851), tower (1889)
Mottram-in -Longdendale	—	nave and clerestory (1854)
Bowdon	—	whole church (1858)
Daresbury	—	part of south aisle (1870)
Northenden	—	body of church (1874)
Chester St. John Baptist	—	north west tower (fell down 1881)
Pulford	—	tower (1833)
Bebington	—	treasury (1897)

Renaissance (1558 to 1660)

The predominant architectural style used through the period was domestic Perpendicular, essentially a simplified or debased form of the late Perpendicular or Tudor. The Perpendicular style which before the commencement of the period (i.e. before 1558) had already shown signs of simplification (such as in the elimination of window-tracery or in a reduction of the ornamentation of capitals), was transformed from a style of architecture that was ecclesiastical into a domestic one. Only at the very end of the period at Upper Peover was there the first manifestation in Cheshire of its replacement by an entirely new and different style, the neo-Classical.

This domestic Perpendicular style is immediately recognised by its windows which are small and set under square heads. Such windows are frequently divided by plain stone mullions into several rectangular lights (such as Burwardsley and Hargrave), and have segmental, elliptical or even straight tops — all uncusped. Sometimes the larger windows are also divided horizontally, that is into two or more rows of sub-lights by plain stone transoms (e.g. Harthill east window). Doorways, too, are plain with shallow Tudor or elliptical heads (e.g. Wincle). Occasionally the doorway is framed in a label. Roofs are steep and gabled, and covered with Kerridge slabs. Their eaves overhang the walls. Internally, roofs display a development in construction with the hammerbeam and arch-brace type predominating (seen to good effect at Harthill or Lower Whitley). Stone mouldings are reduced to simple types such as plain chamfers, simple hollows and rounds.

The Renaissance period in Cheshire is not one from which much fabric has survived, probably because not much was built at that time. What there is is a handful of small new churches, some good roofs and a few pulpits as well as some tombs but not much else.

During the reign of Elizabeth I it is likely that only two small churches were constructed from new, namely at Burleydam and Marple. In the early Stuart or Jacobean period, the position was not much better with three small churches built: Burwardsley (date unknown), Hargrave (1627) and Wincle (1647). Two other churches which had been founded earlier, were completely rebuilt. These were Harthill (1609) and Lower Whitley (1620). One other church, Wybunbury, was completely rebuilt in 1591 apart from its tower.

Hargrave, St. Peter.

In the cases of a few churches, some entirely new sections (mostly mortuary chapels) were built. These sections include Congleton aisles and porch (1613) later destroyed and replaced, Tilston mortuary chapel (1659) and Upper Peover mortuary chapel (1648).

Sections of churches that were rebuilt or repaired include Cheadle south porch (1634), Chester St. John Baptist (patched up and made fit for worship, 1581), Chester St. Michael body and tower (1582) now replaced, Chester St. Peter spire (1580), Farndon body and part of tower badly damaged in the Civil War (1658), Frodsham south chancel chapel (1599), Holmes Chapel south chancel chapel (1589) later destroyed, Lower Peover tower (1582) and chapels (1610 & 1624), Macclesfield St. Michael mortuary chapel (1620). Prestbury south aisle windows (1612), Sandbach oratory chapel (1589) later destroyed, Stockport tower (1616) since replaced, and Warburton Old Church nave (1645).

The work of construction at this time was dominated by the woodcarvers and carpenters, and one of their chief tasks in this Elizabethan and Jacobean period was to renew or repair church roofs. A few roofs treated in this manner survive from the second half of C16 but hardly any in Cheshire can be dated with exactitude. Exceptions are Nantwich (the camber-beam roofs of its transepts carrying the date 1577), Barthomley (nave and aisles, 1589) and Chester cathedral (nave, 1599). The work of renewal was continued in the first half of C17, with instances at Middlewich (chancel, 1621), Tarvin (nave, 1650) and Waverton (nave and aisles, 1635), as well as at the newly constructed churches of Hargrave, Harthill and Lower Whitley. At Rostherne is a rare timber lichgate (1640).

When the timber craftsmen had not got roofs to build, they attended to the fittings and fixtures of churches. Cheshire possesses a series of handsome panelled pulpits including the following dated ones: Stockport St. Mary (a remnant, 1598), Nantwich (1601), Prestbury (1607), Marton (1620), Lymm (1623) and Siddington (1633). Several others belonging to the same period are undated. They include pulpits at Lower Peover, Upper Peover and Daresbury, the latter the most elaborate of the whole group.

Other timber items which were made, though mostly late in the period, include a ringers' gallery at Prestbury (1637), parclose screens at Weaverham (1636) and, possibly, one or two sets of communion rails, for instance at Stoak where there are strong twisted balusters and at Middlewich. There is a rare Jacobean

Rostherne, timber lichgate, 1640.

Daresbury, Jacobean pulpit, early C17.

chancel screen (1609) at Harthill and font covers at Malpas (1627) and Warburton (1595, in new church). The paucity of timber objects other than pulpits (and some furniture) is probably due to the destruction of "popish" objects which undoubtedly took place in Cheshire in Commonwealth times, destruction wrought in a county noted for its adherence to the parliamentary and thus protestant cause.

There are two wooden breadshelves in the county belonging to the period. These are at Mottram-in-Longdendale (1619) and Woodchurch (1641). They are probably all that are left of a fairly large number donated in Jacobean times.

Tombs and memorials: Notwithstanding this orgy of destruction directed against all "superstitious" objects irrespective of whether they had been installed in churches before or after 1540, the most numerous class of fixed artefacts to survive from the Renaissance period are tombs and other memorials, especially those erected between 1600 and 1649. The reason is not hard to explain. As the long Elizabethan reign unfolded giving way to the reigns of the early Stuart kings, monuments were increasingly installed in churches, these often commemorating civic dignitaries and members of the middle classes as well as the landed gentry. Moreover as C16 gave way to C17, the old Gothic — and thus religious or "superstitious" — designs and motifs tended to be replaced on tombs and memorials by new neo-Classical designs and motifs which had a more secular appearance. The outcome was that newly installed monuments did not attract the concentrated attention of parliamentary iconoclasts as did the older ones.

The period is well represented by effigied tombs, but not one survives from the period before 1599. This significant fact suggests that the iconoclasts effectively "cleansed" Cheshire churches of their "popish" monuments. The list of effigied tombs, all displaying neo-Classical influences, include Astbury (lady on table-tomb, 1599), Bowdon (civilian & wife on canopied table-tomb, 1630), Bunbury (knight on canopied table-tomb, +1601 erected 1620), Chester St. Mary (civilian & wife on table-tomb, c.1613; lawyer on table-tomb, 1616), Gawsworth (knight on table-tomb, 1608; knight & lady on table-tomb, 1619; seated lady on table-tomb, 1627; knight & lady on table-tomb, 1643), Macclesfield St. Michael (knight & lady on canopied table-tomb, 1597 erected 1630), Malpas (knight & lady on table-tomb, 1605), Nantwich *formerly at Wybunbury* (knight & lady on canopied table-tomb, 1614) and Upper Peover (knight & lady on table-tomb, 1647). Although one or two of these tombs (for instance Gawsworth) have lost their canopies, the majority are in reasonably good condition. The effigied tomb now at Nantwich is a particularly handsome specimen of the period not always noted for good style or workmanship.

Besides these, there are two canopied table-tombs in the county which appear never to have had effigies. Both have a Gothic appearance, one at Church Lawton (1555) with a very simple design and the other at Over (c.1555). At Baddiley (1631) and Eastham (1612), there are two unadorned table-tombs. Also, there is a now-tombless effigy of a knight (1575) at Great Budworth which is badly mutilated.

The period witnessed the erection of a variety of wall memorials. One group consists of some elaborate compositions with head-and-shoulder likenesses of the deceased in full relief. These include Brereton (civilian & wife, 1643), Chester cathedral (civilian & two wives, 1602) and Chester St. Peter (civilian, 1588). The remainder of these wall memorials form a miscellany, most being tablets. The list includes Brereton (inscribed tablet, 1618), Chester St. John Baptist (inscribed rectangular tablet, 1635), Dodleston (inscribed tablet, 1588), Heswall (inscribed tablet including likeness of a male figure, 1619), Macclesfield St. Michael (incised alabaster tablet, 1552; plain brass plaque, 1589; ditto, 1630; Perkin-a-Legh brass plaque of indeterminate date), Middlewich (brass plaque, 1591), Prestbury (brass plaque, 1589), Tarporley (stone medallion, 1629), Tarvin (brass plaque, 1584) and Upper Peover (plain wooden tablet, 1624).

Another group of wall memorials which are numerous, are the famous Randle Holme wooden heraldic tablets. Designed and made by four generations of that family, the tablets were placed in churches of Cheshire and North Wales. All the Cheshire churches containing these tablets lie on the western side of the county, except for Chelford and Knutsford. The tablets which number fifty seven in Cheshire, date mainly from C17, but a few are as late as the early years of C18. The tablets form a homogeneous group and the later ones, although outside the period under present discussion, are included in the following list: The tablets are distributed in eighteen churches, i.e. Audlem 4, Backford 6, Baddiley 1, Bunbury 1, Chelford 1, Chester cathedral 3, Chester St. John Baptist 9, Chester St. Peter 2, Church Minshull 1, Farndon 2, Guilden Sutton 1, Knutsford 1, Plemstall 1, Stoak 11, Tarvin 3, Thornton-le-Moors 6, Woodchurch 3 and Wrenbury 1. The tablets which may be regarded as forerunners of the common C18 hatchment, are characterised by display of the deceased's achievement and a statement of his family connections.

Other memorials of the period include a small number of ledger-stones, these being at Daresbury (1634), Dodleston (inlaid marble, 1617) and Tarporley (1646). However, this short list should not be taken as exhaustive as there may be others hidden under carpets, pews, etc. In two churches, Prestbury (1572) and Upper Peover (1573 and 1586), are incised slabs of stone which each portray a knight and his lady, closely resembling the incised slabs of the preceding Perpendicular period. Lastly, there is the brass memorial which forms part of the Starkey plain table-tomb of c.1555 at Winsford.

Special mention should be made of the timber heraldic screens at Middlewich. Unique in Cheshire, they were installed in 1632 and 1633 in memory of the Venables family.

Stoneware: Because of the prevailing religious climate little new work was commissioned in Cheshire churches except for a small number of fonts. Though it is doubtful whether any were made in the C16 Elizabethan period, at least two fonts survive from the first half of C17 at Guilden Sutton (dated 1635), and Warburton Old Church (dated 1603).

Stained glass: Virtually no glass survives from this time. One or two churches, however, possess foreign glass of the period that was installed relatively recently. Birtles has some C17 glass from the Nederlands; while at Woodchurch are eight Flemish medallions of c.1650.

As the period did not involve much construction, the record of destroyed work is correspondingly small. The list includes:—

Frodsham — south chancel chapel 1599 (destroyed and rebuilt 1724 and again in 1882)

Congleton — two lean-to aisles and south porch 1613 (destroyed 1741 when body of church was rebuilt)

Wybunbury — body of church 1591 (destroyed and rebuilt in 1836 and since pulled down)

Bunbury — Elizabethan clerestory (destroyed and replaced 1864)

Daresbury — south porch 1628 (destroyed and rebuilt 1870-72)

Warmingham — south porch 1620 (destroyed 1870).

Post-Restoration and Neo-Classical (1660 to 1820)

The last years of C17 following the return from exile of Charles II were a transitional phase for church architecture in which there was a carry-over of the domestic style that had dominated the pre-Commonwealth period. These post-Restoration years which for practical purposes may be taken as lasting until the end of the century, were not a period when much rebuilding or new construction was going on in Cheshire. Two small churches which had their origins in late C17 are Macclesfield Forest (built 1673, restored 1834) and Tushingham Old Church which though having a medieval history, was completely rebuilt in 1689-91. Constructed of brick, this second building which is typical of a small rural church of its period, is completely unaltered, displaying simplicity and quaintness. It has a gabled roof with overhanging eaves, a mixture of square-headed and semi-circular headed windows, and fittings and fixtures which also date from 1691.

Tushingham Old Church, St. Chad.

Some rebuilding and repair of churches did take place, this being partly due to damage caused in the Civil War. Acton, one of the casualties, had its fabric made good in 1680, including its chancel which received an elaborate pierced parapet. Another piece of reconstruction following accidental damage involved the south chancel chapel at Chester St. Mary (1693). It is also likely that the nave of Chadkirk received treatment c.1660, but whether this was a new construction or patch-up job is not known.

A small number of other minor building jobs were done between 1660 and 1700, but it is not certain whether they were all replacements for older fabric. Instances include the south porch at Thornton-le-Moors of c.1700, and the south aisle chapel at Wilmslow of similar date.

In post-Restoration times most attention was directed towards ameliorating the excessive damage and decay suffered by churches following a century or more of neglect and making them fit for worship again. In this campaign of reconstruction the woodworkers were foremost, much of their output surviving to the present day. Numerically, altar-rails are the most common items, with good examples at Acton (flat balusters, 1685), Astbury (Dutch strapwork design, undated), Burton (alternating turned and twisted balusters, undated), Frodsham (twisted balusters, c.1700), Ince (twisted balusters, undated), Lower Peover (turned balusters, undated), Shotwick (turned balusters, undated) Stoak (twisted balusters, undated), Thornton-le-Moors (twisted balusters, c.1694) and Tilston (flat balusters, 1677).

Many of the box-pews of the period have been turned out of the churches but examples remain at Astbury (early), Baddiley (c.1700), Malpas (1680) and Wrenbury (a set with coats of arms on the doors, c.1700). A few churches too have churchwardens' pews, namely Macclesfield St. Michael (early), Plemstall (1697) and Shotwick (1673). There is some panelling belonging to the period but not as much as might have been expected. Dated examples are found at Guilden Sutton (1698) in the form of an arch, Taxal (1694) and Thornton-le-Moors (1694). Much of the woodwork of the chancel of Lower Peover also originates in late C17. There are two half-screens at Acton (1685) and Warburton (late C17) and a gallery screen at Mobberley (1683). Two font covers of note are located at Astbury (undated) and Bunbury (1663).

Other pieces of timberwork include a pulpit (Shocklach, 1687), reredos (Barthomley, late C17, now in tower), bible boxes (Burton, late C17; and Disley, 1693), poor box (Middlewich, 1682), the

Lower Peover, timbered interior to east, C14 and C17.

Stanley pew (Nether Alderley, late C17), breadshelves (Woodchurch, 1670) and a three-decker pulpit (Baddiley, c.1700).

Roof rebuilding also continued throughout the period in order to make good the neglect, with prominent examples at Sandbach (nave, 1661), Handley (nave, 1661, an attractive hammerbeam instance), Great Barrow (chancel, 1671) Ince (chancel, 1671), and Prestbury (nave, 1674, a crude piece of work originally plastered or intended to be plastered).

The county is sparsely endowed with stone artefacts installed in post-Restoration days. The chief type are fonts nearly all of which are plain and octagonal. Three of them are dated: Brereton (1660), Bunbury (1663) and Thornton-le-Moors (1673). One or two others have classical designs, notably Chester St. Peter (oval shape, 1662) and Chester cathedral (1687).

Churchyard sundials began to appear about this time. The majority were crude adaptations of medieval crosses which were truncated and topped. However, one or two sundials were purpose-built, a handsome instance being at Prestbury (1672).

The county possesses a number of Royal arms almost all of which are painted on boards or canvas. An exception is that at Baddiley to Charles II dated 1663, which is painted on the medieval tympanum over the entrance to the chancel. Although Royal arms were displayed in churches as early as 1541 elsewhere, none survive in Cheshire from before 1660 (e.g. to Charles II at Whitegate). Other good examples of the period all showing the arms of Charles II, may be seen at Astbury (undated), Bunbury (1661, repainted 1730), Upper Peover (1661) and Waverton (1663). The Royal arms of Charles II at Neston consist of carved wood which is painted and gilded.

Benefaction or charity boards became fairly numerous in the period and a few Cheshire churches have them. A particularly handsome example (1689) is at Tushingham Old Church.

The period does not retain as many memorials as might have been expected, possibly due to the fact that a lot of them were swept away in C19 during church restorations as at Nantwich. Free-standing effigied table-tombs in keeping with medieval and Renaissance practices were becoming rare in this period, and

Baddiley, medieval tympanum repainted with Royal arms and texts, etc., 1663.

there are only a few in Cheshire churches: at Acton (Sir Richard Wilbraham +1643 and wife +c.1660), Cheadle (Sir Thomas Brereton +1673) and Tarporley (Mary Crewe +1690). Besides these there are one or two table-tombs unadorned by effigies (Barthomley, Sir Christopher Turnor +1693; and Eastham, Charlotte Lady Stanley +1662). Also in churchyards at Aston-by-Sutton (John Okell +1697) and Taxal (Elizabeth Shallcross +c.1682) there are effigy-less table-tombs. A trend which accelerated in C18 was for big memorials to be stood on the floor against walls, and there are occasional instances in the county notably an excellent one at Macclesfield St. Michael which consists of a table-tomb on which rests the semi-reclining bewigged figure of Earl Rivers +1694 (by W. Stanton). Another at Bowdon displays the Earl of Warrington +1693 (by André Carpentière).

There are several high quality and elaborately fashioned wall tablets with examples at Chester St. John Baptist (Diana Warburton +1693, with skeleton, by Edward Pearce), Lower Peover (Sir Geoffrey Shakerley +1696) and the cathedral (Sir William Mainwaring +1671). A variant of wall tablet is the cartouche of which two specimens deserve mention (Chester St. John Baptist, Edward Harbert +1688; and Stoak, Henry Bunbury +1664, the latter arguably the most beautiful memorial in the county). A simpler wall memorial in the form of an armorial panel below an open pediment to Katherine Glegg +1666, is at Heswall. Plain stone wall tablets of the forty year period are scarce (e.g. West Kirby, Johannes Vanzoelen +1689). However, there are a number of small and usually rectangular shaped copper and brass wall and floor plaques (as at Grappenhall, Lower Peover, Malpas and Wrenbury). Ledger-stones set in the floor are relatively few (e.g. Taxal) and nearly all of them are plain with large and crude lettering.

Apart from Randle Holme heraldic tablets which overlap into this post-Restoration period and which have already been described, few other memorials are made of wood. One is at Mobberley where there is a curious painted board to Elizabeth and Nathaniel Robinson (dated 1665).

There is little stained glass, an example being at Farndon (mid C17) which shows some Civil War scenes. There is almost no wrought-iron work.

Given the small amount of construction and reconstruction work in post-Restoration days, not surprisingly only little of this work is recorded as having been destroyed in C18 or C19. The list

Aston, table-tomb in churchyard of John Okell + 1697.

Aston, inscription on top of same tomb.

includes Chester Holy Trinity (part rebuilt 1679), Chester St. Bridget (rebuilt c.1680 and permanently demolished C19), Christleton (part rebuilt 1678), Davenham (chancel and spire rebuilt 1680), Goostrey (south aisle built 1668) and Halton (rebuilt 1670).

We now move to the main part of the period, that is from 1701 to 1820. This was of lengthy duration when the neo-Classical style was dominant. Construction was mainly undertaken using brick, though some churches were built of ashlar. Sometimes facings such as quoins, strings and cills were made of stone. Windows normally had semi-circular heads below which was thin tracery. Quoins were frequently rusticated. Parapets on roofs and towers were plain or balustraded, some being topped with spheres or simple pinnacles. Buildings especially towers had heavy strings of brick or stone. Doorways were square-headed and framed in flanking pilasters or columns, often with triangular pediments.

The floor-plan tended to consist of a wide nave which may have been aisled in the larger churches. Almost invariably the tower was at the west end. The chancel was shallow and apsidal, consisting of not much more than a sanctuary. Internally, arcades tended towards having plain semi-circular arches and round or square piers. Churches were filled with galleries and box-pews. To see the congregation above the high sides and fronts of the pews and to look into the galleries, preachers would speak from three-decker pulpits. Roofs were normally plastered with moulded and panelled ceilings.

By the start of C18 the accumulated neglect of many churches throughout the land including Cheshire could not be avoided. Some buildings were so badly decayed (such as Burton and Church Minshull) that they needed virtually to be re-erected. Not infrequently medieval towers had become unsafe, made worse by storms, lightning etc. And occasionally (as at Rostherne), they actually fell down. Another factor was that the form of religion had changed since the Reformation with emphasis now on the Spoken Word. It was widely felt that many churches should be converted into rectangular, galleried preaching houses. In this scheme long medieval chancels tended to become redundant reverting to use by the local nobility or gentry as mortuary chapels (e.g. Nantwich) where they would be filled by Georgian tombs.

In the light of these considerations it was often cheaper to pull down existing churches and rebuild from scratch than to convert such buildings, this preferred policy being enthusiastically practised up and down the county. The rise of population in towns affected by the Industrial Revolution (notably Macclesfield and Stockport) created a genuine need for new churches especially in districts where there had been none before. Thus the second half of C18 as well as much of the succeeding century saw a steady increase in the founding of such buildings.

Generally speaking, church design in Cheshire between 1701 and 1820 was not of a high standard. There were a few exceptions however, almost all being greater churches. Two in particular, Alsager Christ Church and Knutsford St. John Baptist, have dignified exteriors; while the last-named church together with Congleton have interesting and well-proportioned interiors. Of the smaller buildings, Somerford which commenced life as a domestic chapel of the Shakerleys, is deserving of mention for its outside appearance, and Church Minshull for its interior. The majority of churches rebuilt or partly rebuilt were small and generally unpleasing in their external views. This was largely due to the fact that most were constructed by local contractors whose knowledge of church building was limited to speculative house construction. Using dull grey brick — a cheap material to hand — and designs which made churches look like rectangular boxes (e.g. Saltersford Jenkin Chapel, Macclesfield Christ Church), builders in Cheshire failed to reach standards that were being attained elsewhere. Moreoever in those churches where partial rebuilding had occured, frequently the neo-Classical work failed to blend with the old work, for instance at Rostherne where the C18 tower though well proportioned in its own right, is totally out of keeping with the body of the church, or at Bosley where a new body was grafted on to a medieval tower.

Ten entirely new churches were built in the period, these being Somerford (1725), Saltersford Jenkin Chapel (1733), Knutsford St. John Baptist (1741-44, a replacement for Knutsford St. Helena demolished on another site), Carrington (1757-59), Stockport St. Peter (1768), Macclesfield Christ Church (1775-76), Alsager Christ Church (1789-90), Altrincham St. George (1799), Threapwood (1815) and Delamere (1816-17). All of these buildings largely survive, though Altrincham was reconstructed piecemeal by the Victorians in at least three campaigns.

A number of ancient churches were completely rebuilt between 1701 and 1820. These include Woodhead (C18, exact date unknown), Ashton-on-Mersey (1714), Chester Little St. John (1717, rebuilt as part of the former Bluecoat School), Burleydam (1769), Chelford (1776), Goostrey (1792-96), Haslington (1809-10) and Guilden Sutton (1815).

Congleton, neo-Classical interior to east, 1742.

Yet another group of ancient churches had substantial portions of their fabrics rebuilt between 1701 and 1820. The list of those whose fabrics survive to the present (with dates of their rebuilding, 1701-1820, given in brackets) are:—

Holmes Chapel	—	nave encased (c.1700); chancel (c.1732)
Church Minshull	—	tower (1702); body (1704)
Warburton Old Church	—	tower and chancel (1711)
Warmingham	—	tower (1715)
Burton	—	tower, nave and north aisle (1721)
Swettenham	—	tower, body encased (1721-22)
Upper Peover	—	tower (1739-41); nave and chancel (1811)
Congleton	—	body (1740-42); upper part of tower (1786)
Rostherne	—	tower (1742-44)

Great Barrow	—	tower, south wall of nave (1744)
Chadkirk	—	south side of nave (1747)
Bosley	—	body (1777)
Burwardsley	—	most of building (1795)
Little Budworth	—	body (1800)
Mellor	—	body (early C19)
Church Lawton	—	body (1803)
Wrenbury	—	chancel (1806)
Baddiley	—	nave encased (1811)
Stockport St. Mary	—	tower, nave and aisles (1813-17)
Siddington	—	nave encased (c.1815)

The chancels of Marton and Tarvin were rebuilt in C18, the second largely reconstructed again in 1891-92.

In the case of a few churches, some smaller portions which were assembled in C18 or early C19 as replacements or additions, survive. These include two porches at Frodsham (1715 and 1724), a vestry believed to have been designed by Sir John Vanbrugh at Malpas (1717), and a porch at Farndon (1814).

As the period unfolded there was a trend towards the reintroduction of Gothic features in buildings. This started with the employment of thin tracery — often of the Y-type — in windows (e.g. Taxal), and with pointed window-arches (e.g. Baddiley) rather than semi-circular ones. Also in a few churches where neo-Classical characteristics had been introduced, Gothic features were substituted in the Victorian era (so-called "regothicisation") usually by the replacement of round-topped windows with pointed ones. Thus Warmingham tower was regothicised in 1899, Wrenbury chancel in 1865, and Marbury chancel in 1891-92.

Victorian restorers often took the view that rather than regothicise, it was less trouble to knock down offending sections of churches and rebuild such sections in their entirety. A typical example of where this was done is Backford nave built 1728-31 in the neo-Classical style (pictured in detail in a C19 photograph of

Warmingham, neo-Classical tower of 1715, regothicised 1899.

Backford, old photograph showing church before 1879 when the nave was rebuilt.

the church) and rebuilt in 1879 in neo-Gothic. Another instance is Frodsham where the south aisle constructed in 1724 at the same time as the surviving south porch, was replaced by a neo-Gothic aisle in 1882. At Whitegate the medieval body of the church was largely rebuilt in 1728, and when this section was rebuilt yet again in 1874-75 the neo-Classical south doorway of the nave was retained. At Eccleston the small church built in 1809-13 was replaced by a magnificent large church in 1899 by G.F. Bodley on an adjacent site in the churchyard, a ruined wall of the older building surviving.

The list of churches or sections of churches rebuilt or constructed between 1701 and 1820 which were rebuilt by the Victorians, is quite lengthy. The major work includes:—

Chester Holy Trinity	—	(1728 & 1774) rebuilt 1865-69
Macclesfield St. Michael	—	nave and aisles (1740) chancel (1819) all rebuilt 1901
Prestbury	—	north aisle (1740) rebuilt 1879
Runcorn	—	south aisle (1740) rebuilt 1847-49
Wallasey	—	body (1759) rebuilt as new church on adjacent site in churchyard 1858-59

Daresbury	—	chancel (1795) rebuilt 1870-72
Warmingham	—	body (1797) rebuilt 1870
Guilden Sutton	—	chancel (1802) rebuilt 1815
Marple	—	body (1808-12) rebuilt as new church on adjacent site in churchyard 1878-80.

Other churches of the period, mostly small, which were replaced in C19 in their entirety include Little Legh (1720), Ringway now redundant (1720), Staleybridge (1776), Thelwall (1782) and High Legh (1814-18). A few other churches were destroyed and not rebuilt, i.e. Chester St. Martin (1721), Poynton (1787) and Overchurch (1813), the last two being replaced by churches on new sites.

Stoneware: Apart from monumental masonry, little stoneware was introduced into Cheshire churches during C18 and early C19. The only exception was fonts of which the chief design was the gadrooned round bowl with baluster stem. Occasionally such fonts were painted (e.g. Little Budworth), and in one or two instances marble was used (as at Congleton, 1742). Other examples of fonts of this neo-Classical type are at Chadkirk (C18), Church Minshull (1717), Macclesfield St. Michael (1744), Knutsford St. John Baptist (1741), Northenden (C18), Swettenham (C18) and Thornton-le-Moors (C18). In addition there are a few octagonal fonts of the period (e.g. Great Barrow, 1713).

In churchyards there are some sundials of the period with baluster stems (for instance Rostherne, 1772; Warburton Old Church, 1765). Generally, these sundials are more stylish in appearance than the far more numerous sundials made from truncated medieval crosses.

Woodwork: By far the greatest number of artefacts are made of timber rather than stone. Altar-rails are the biggest group with their turned balusters tending towards a heavier and possibly plainer looking style as C18 progressed. Churches with such balusters include Bruera (C18), Bunbury (c.1717), Congleton (Laudian rails, C18), Guilden Sutton (early C18), Plemstall (early C18), Pott Shrigley (C18), Shocklach (C18), Swettenham (Laudian rails, C18) and Weaverham (1708). Sometimes as at Baddiley (1701) the rails are flat balusters, a hangover from the previous century.

There are some timber pulpits, well proportioned in a Georgian style with strong panelling. Instances are found at Goostrey (early

Little Budworth, neo-Classical font, C18.

C19), Harthill (C18), Little Budworth (c.1800), Swettenham (early C18), Tilston (early C18) and Wrenbury (c.1800). A timber pulpit that is said to have come from Astbury, stands in the middle of the central aisle at Congleton (C18). In addition, there are two three-decker pulpits — at Plemstall (1722) and Shotwick (1812). Also at the last church is a rare wooden lectern (late C18).

The churches have some fittings, but one suspects that many were swept away in the High Victorian frenzy of restoration. Thus there are some box-pews at Shotwick (c.1706), Mellor (C18) and Weaverham (early C18). Wrenbury possesses the famous "dog whipper's pew" dated 1734, and Prestbury has some churchwardens' pews dated 1707. The latter church also possesses two rare screens of the period, one leading into the chancel (1787) and the other dividing the north aisle from the north chancel chapel (1744). There is an instance of oak panelling at Holmes Chapel (1732) where it is used to furnish the chancel. Several west galleries remain, with instances at Ashton-on-Mersey (1743), Baddiley (C18), Chelford (1776), Congleton (1748), Goostrey (1792), Haslington (c.1810), Holmes Chapel (1705), Knutsford St. John Baptist (1744), Nether Alderley (1801), Siddington (1786), and Wrenbury (late C18). Breadshelves survive at Lower Peover (1720 & 1739), Thurstaston (1723) and Mottram-in-Longdendale (1737). Almost all reredoses were swept away by the Victorians, two or three surviving of which the best at Congleton (1743) is panelled with a pelican carving.

Metalwork: The chief introduction into churches consisted of brass chandeliers at the beginning of C18, nearly all of which are two-tiered. There are a number of examples in Cheshire, the earliest of which is at Holmes Chapel (1708). There are uncommon chandeliers at Shotwick (undated C18, single-tiered) and Frodsham (1805, three-tiered). Macclesfield St. Michael is filled with chandeliers, the oldest dated 1739. Other chandeliers are located at Ince (1724), Knutsford St. John Baptist (1763), Marple (1811), Prestbury (1712 and 1814) and Tattenhall (1755).

There are some sets of wrought-iron gates at the entrance to churchyards of which two magnificent pairs are at Malpas (early C18). Another pair is at Eccleston (also early C18)[1]. There are two single-handed clocks in Cheshire both of the period, one at Stoak and the other at Burton. There are also some two-handed turret clocks (e.g. Little Budworth, 1728 and Stockport St. Peter, 1769).

There are a number of Royal arms, most of which are of George III and are constructed of painted boards or canvas. Examples are

Stoak tower, single-handed clock, C18.

at Goostrey, Heswall and Runcorn. At Stockport the arms of the same king (1813) are modelled in plaster. Other monarchs represented are William III (1702) at Congleton, Queen Anne (c.1702-14) at Grappenhall, and George I (1726) at Shotwick.

In C18 and early C19 churches were often equipped with two large boards on which were written the Ten Commandments, Apostles' Creed and Lord's Prayer, etc. Many of these boards remain, for example at Eastham where the "boards" appear to consist of sheets of iron, and Tarvin. Originally the boards were designed to hang on either side of the east window of the chancel. But in many churches they have been consigned to inferior positions such as the west end (as at Eastham) or the north aisle (as at Shotwick). Occasionally religious figures were painted on the boards, and one or two survive (for instance Moses and Aaron at Marton, and St. Peter and St. Paul at Congleton, both sets by Edward Penny[2]).

Memorials: Stone in its many and varied types was almost universally used between 1701 and 1820 for tombs, tablets, etc. Occasionally, brass was used for small rectangular plaques (as at

Weaverham: Thomas Pierson 1762 & Daniel Milner 1779). Timber was used for some hatchments (e.g. Church Lawton).

There are a few really large C18 memorials in the county, but probably not as many as might have been anticipated. Normally located close to the wall, memorials of this kind generally consist of a table above which is a wall section. The two grandest are at Bowdon and Rostherne. The former is by André Carpentière to Langham Booth +1724, and the latter (1792) by Bacon to Samuel Egerton +1780. Another at Tarporley which has lost its canopy shows an effigy of Sir John Crewe +1711 lying on a table-tomb. A fourth at Mottram-in-Longdendale commemorates Reginald Breckland +1703, his bewigged effigy displayed in an uncomfortable posture.

A number of churches possess wall memorials some of which are quite elaborate (e.g. Northenden, Mary Egerton +1784: Stockport St. Peter, William Wright +1770; Wrenbury, Sir Lynch Cotton +1775). Others include the memorials at Baddiley (to Sir Thomas Mainwaring +1726), Prestbury (to Richard Orford +1791, and another to Charles Legh +1781). and at Chester St. Mary (to members of the Randle Holme family, early C18). But other wall memorials are quite plain (such as Stockport St. Mary to John Wainwright +1768; and Waverton to William Dutton +1762). The wall cartouche was sometimes used in C18, a refined example being found at Warmingham (to William Vernon +1732).

The most frequently occurring memorial of the period found in Cheshire churches is the ledger-stone. In contrast to that of the previous century, the incised lettering is of high quality.

The period was one when many charitable bequests were made, these recorded on benefaction boards attached to the inner walls of churches. Examples include Warmingham (1755) and Acton (a very large board covering the years 1786-1789).

---

[1]All these were probably the work of the famous Davies brothers of Bersham, North Wales, who were productive in the first half of C18.
[2]Edward Penny who was a native of Knutsford, was a founder member of the Royal Academy.

8. Churches with Grouped Features

As in other parts of England, features involving design and use of materials tend to repeat in groups of churches in Cheshire. And moreover, these groups often correspond with particular geographical areas of the county. Five such groups may be identified, namely:—

a) THE TWO-AISLED CHURCHES
In the Chester area are seven churches which possess a nave and north aisle. These are Burton, Chester St. Michael, Dodleston, Great Barrow, Ince, Plemstall and Shotwick. A type of building surviving nowhere else in Cheshire, it is still found frequently in Clwyd and Shropshire. The two-aisled church was developed from the single-aisled type[1] common in C11 and C12. The north side tended to be selected for an additional aisle as the ground on that side of the building would have been unpopular for burials and therefore little used for that purpose.

Two of the churches, Shotwick and Plemstall, conform to a variety of the two-aisled type which is found in the Vale of Clwyd. Here, the arrangements comprise two aisles or naves of approximately equal width running side by side without structural division (i.e. there are no archways separating chancel from nave or north chancel chapel from north aisle). The two through-components are separated by a six-bay arcade.

At Thornton-le-Moors there is a two-aisled church with the side-aisle, less commonly, situated to the south of the nave. Given that the lay-out of this building was altered by structural changes made at the west and east ends in C16 and C19, the church can claim affinities with the Vale of Clwyd model, notably in having two aisles of approximately equal width. Woodchurch which since 1965, has been three-aisled, may also have had affinities with the two-aisled type. Like Thornton-le-Moors its ancient aisle, originally constructed in C14, is on the south side.

b) THE TIMBER-FRAMED CHURCHES
Throughout the later medieval period (C14, C15 & C16) small timber-framed churches were erected, undoubtedly because timber was readily available, especially in the

Coppenhall, former timber-framed church of C16, demolished 1821.

forested parts of Cheshire. The ease of hauling oak trunks minor distances compared with transporting loads of good quality stone from further afield, obviously was an important factor in minimising costs.

Evidence is scanty as to which churches of the group in the county were originally fully timbered. It is known that at least one, Church Coppenhall, did survive in this form until recent times. With the exception of Whitegate of which only the timber piers of its medieval arcades are extant, members of the group retain some half-timbered features only in their respective fabrics. Not a single building can claim to be half-timbered in its entirety now. Nearly all are located in the centre and east of the county. The list comprises Baddiley, Chadkirk, Holmes Chapel, Lower Peover, Marton, Siddington, Swettenham, Warburton Old Church and Whitegate.

The two buildings which are most complete are Lower Peover and Marton, the former having a stone tower and the latter a brick chancel. Four (Baddiley, Holmes Chapel, Siddington and Swettenham) had their naves encased in brick after the Reformation. Chadkirk and Warburton retain

Northenden, demolished except for tower, 1874.

only small sections of their medieval half-timbering. Difficult though it is to be precise, it is likely that the surviving timberwork of Baddiley, Chadkirk, Lower Peover, Marton, Swettenham and Warburton date from C14; whilst Holmes Chapel which possesses a complex roof-structure, and Whitegate date from C15. Siddington probably dates from early C16.

c) THE EAST CHESHIRE CHURCHES
Several ancient churches in the east of the county have common characteristics, viz:—

*steep gabled roofs of nave, chancel and aisles clad with Kerridge slabs
*walls with overhanging eaves (instead of embattled or plain parapets)
*square-headed windows of three lights along the walls of aisles
*clerestories which create the impression of being long and low
*square-headed windows of two lights along the walls of the clerestories.

The churches belonging to this group are Cheadle, Farndon, Grappenhall, Mobberley, Nether Alderley, Prestbury, Rostherne and Wilmslow. Several other churches which suffered grieviously at the hands of Victorian restorers, as evidence from early photographs, etc. shows, used to belong to the group (notably Bowdon and Northenden).

Except possibly for Farndon, they were all reconstructed in early C16, being given clerestories and aisles with square-headed windows. Those buildings which conform most closely to the style are Mobberley, Nether Alderley and Prestbury. Farndon at the opposite end of the county, was restored after the Civil War having been badly damaged, and any similarity of this church to the type must be regarded as coincidental.

In a somewhat restrained way, this group of churches though not to be compared with those of the west Cheshire type, possess dignity and charm. Built of local materials, they fit well into their immediate environments and enhance their surroundings.

d) THE WEST CHESHIRE CHURCHES

Stylistically speaking, the buildings of this group are the most exciting and satisfying of all the churches in the county, the type spilling over the borders into North Wales (especially Gresford, Mold and Wrexham) and the southern part of Lancashire (for instance Sefton and Winwick). The churches are located in a large tract of Cheshire to the west of a line drawn through Great Budworth running from Gawsworth to Daresbury. Unlike the east Cheshire group, these churches were not excessively savaged by C19 restorers, and nearly every one has survived with its medieval fabric largely intact.

The complete list of buildings comprises Acton, Astbury, Audlem, Barthomley, Bebington, Brereton, Bunbury, Chester St. Mary, Gawsworth, Great Budworth, Holt, Malpas, Marbury, Middlewich, Nantwich, Over, Sandbach, Tarvin, Weaverham, Witton and Wrenbury, making twenty one altogether.

Writing in the Journal of the Chester Archaeological Society, Fred Crossley suggested the reason why these superb churches were created out of earlier and in some cases quite modest buildings: "... the love of spaciousness and light and the opportunity it afforded for the display of stained glass"[2]. Sadly though, almost all this late medieval glass has been lost.

The Perpendicular reconstruction of this group of churches which lasted from c.1475 to c.1558 resulted in their having a high clerestory with obtusely arched windows often set closely together, each being normally of four main lights with heads that are four-centred, and elliptical or segmental. The end-windows of the chancel and chancel chapels are similar to those of the aisle-windows, but are of five lights. The roofs are flattened and supported by camber-beams, and are hidden externally by panelled and embattled parapets. The side-walls are supported by deep projecting buttresses between the windows. The tower is normally made higher in order to conform to the new side-elevation of the nave clerestories.

None of the above twenty one churches meets these descriptive criteria in every respect, the closest being Malpas and Great Budworth, both having retained some windows installed in the previous C14 Decorated period.

e) THE RENAISSANCE CHURCHES

The little group of churches built or rebuilt in C17 and referred to earlier, are located to the south and east of Chester and may thus be regarded as belonging to a geographical group. They include Burwardsley, Great Barrow (listed as a two-aisled church too), Hargrave, Harthill and Lower Whitley. These churches are all mainly constructed of stone, are small and have steeply gabled roofs and overhanging eaves. Their windowing reflects the dominant architectural trend of the period. Thus each window has three or four lights under a square head, the tops of the lights being semi-circular or segmental. The churches that correspond most closely with this format are Hargrave and Harthill.

MISCELLANEOUS CHURCHES

Of a possible ninety two churches which possess fabrics surviving from before the Restoration, forty one cannot be allotted to the above five groups. Of these last churches, fifteen have been completely rebuilt save for their medieval towers within the last three hundred or so years. The remaining twenty six differ widely in their design and appearance and in their geographical distribution, thus defying categorisation. They include three major buildings of outstanding historical and architectural merit, namely the cathedral and the parish churches of Chester St. John Baptist and Macclesfield St. Michael. The twenty six also include a number of other important churches notably Eastham, Frodsham, Tarporley and West Kirby. And when we focus our attention on those many other churches which have been built or completely reconstructed since the Restoration, they too display a variety of characteristics as do the older churches of this "group".

Astbury, low-side (or leper) window (c.1290) in north wall of north chancel chapel.

---

[1]Tilston and Handley may be examples of single-aisled churches in the same area which never developed beyond this state.
[2]Crossley, F.H. (1940) "The renaissance of Cheshire church building in the late fifteenth and early sixteenth centuries". In *Journal of the Chester Archaeological Society*, Vol.XXXIV, Pt.II, p.57.

9. A Summary of Some of the Best Features of Cheshire Churches

Beauty, it is said, is in the eye of the beholder. It would therefore be surprising if the list offered below were acceptable to every reader. Also in some cases, "best features" includes items of particular historic interest though not necessarily the most beautiful. The list represents a concensus of opinion and should provide starting points for those visitors who have a limited amount of time to spend touring the county.

Settings	Barthomley, Gawsworth, Marbury, Rostherne, Whitegate.
Exteriors	Astbury, Great Budworth, Malpas.
Towers	Tarvin, Wybunbury.
Interiors	Norman: Chester St. John Baptist (nave and interstitium). Early English: Chester cathedral (lady chapel, vestibule & chapter-house). Decorated: Nantwich (chancel). Perpendicular: Astbury (nave, chancel & west porch), Bebington (east end). neo-Classical: Congleton (body), Knutsford (body).
Canopied stalls	Chester cathedral, Nantwich.
Chests	Malpas.
Fonts	Norman: Mellor. Perpendicular: Holt. neo-Classical: Congleton, Macclesfield St. Michael.
Monuments	Aston-by-Sutton, Macclesfield St. Michael, Stoak, Upper Peover.
Organ cases	Chester cathedral, Bidston.
Pulpits:	stone: Nantwich. wooden: Daresbury, Marbury, Mellor.
Roofs	Astbury, Disley, Witton.

Screens	stone: Bunbury. wooden: Astbury, Mobberley. tympanum: Baddiley.
Sedilia/ Piscinas	Nantwich, Stockport St. Mary.
Stained glass	Birtles, Disley.
Timber fittings/ Fixtures	Lower Peover, Tushingham Old Church.

Astbury, chancel screen, c.1500.

10. The Individual Churches

Below is shown the generalised plan of a parish church on which are labelled the main parts. In the individual descriptions of Cheshire churches which follow, the location of the parts referred to in the texts may be identified from the plan:—

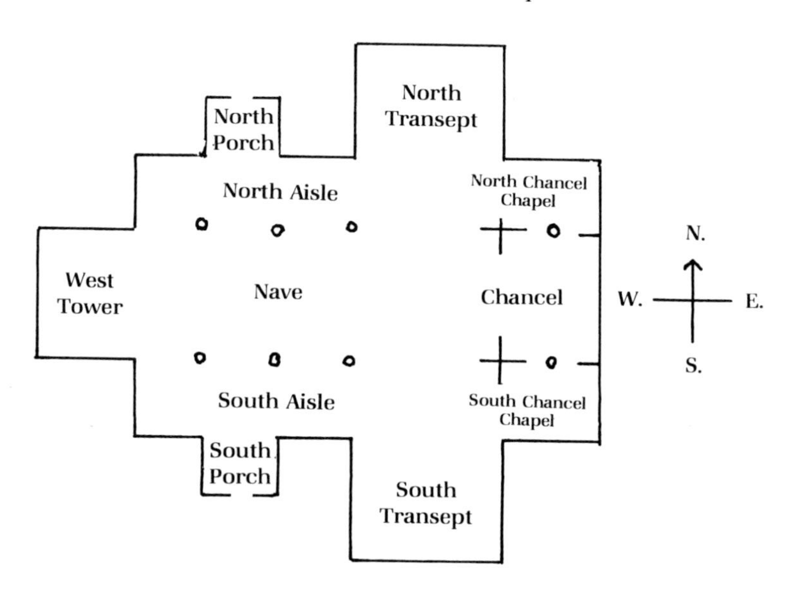

Abbreviations used in the texts

n., s., e., w.	north, south, east, west
ne., nw.	north east, north west
se., sw.	south east, south west
c.	circa (meaning approximately)
C13, C14 etc.	the thirteenth century, the fourteenth century etc.
Norm.	Norman
EE.	Early English
Dec.	Decorated
Perp.	Perpendicular

The numbers shown above each title is the map reference.

631531
ACTON, St. Mary

A large impressive church in a small and unspoilt estate village, it boasts the oldest tower in Cheshire (apart from one at the cathedral). Dating from C13, it possesses EE. thin pilasters and lancet windows on its w. side. Also, the tower which is embraced, has three EE. internal archways, two of which display dogtooth mouldings. The nave arcade piers are C13 EE. as well, but it is likely that they were made higher in later medieval times. With the exception of the tower and the C14 Dec. Dorfold chapel, the church was largely rebuilt in late C14/early C15 in keeping with a style of architecture illustrating the change from Dec. to Perp. In the n. aisle is located the well preserved wall-tomb of Sir William Mainwaring +1399. In the Woodhey chapel at the e. end of the s. aisle is a marble table-tomb on which lie the effigies of Sir Richard Wilbraham +1643 and his wife +c.1660. Nearby are some C11 Norm. carved blocks of stone thought to have belonged to an earlier building on the site. On these blocks are shown God the Father under an arch, a bishop without a mitre, a figure holding a column, two groups of apostles or saints, an eagle, and some interlaced ribbonwork Other artefacts of special interest are an early C18 sundial (possibly the largest in Cheshire), a C12 Norm. font of black basalt, and a very big C18 benefaction board. An unusual feature of the building are the medieval stone benches, installed for the weak and elderly, which line the side walls.

419595
ALDFORD, St. John Baptist

The church was totally rebuilt in a neo-EE. style by J. Douglas in 1866 at the expense of the second marquess of Westminster. In the churchyard, there survives the base of the medieval cross now

Acton, tomb of Sir William Mainwairing +1399.

restored with a new top-section. Nearby is a sundial (1708). There is a medieval stone with a Latin inscription over the s. doorway. A handsome benefaction board covers the period 1682-1723. The church contains several C18 and C19 memorials including a wooden tablet to Frances Jones +1719.

789556
ALSAGER, Christ Church

This dignified Georgian building is located in the centre of the village near the college of higher education, where it was constructed in 1789-90 to a design by Thomas Stringer. It is built in ashlar and has a w. tower the doorway of which possesses Tuscan columns and a pediment. Internally, the chief items of interest are three memorial plaques which record the passing of five "Ladies of the Manor of Alsager", members of the Alsager family who met the cost of building the church. In the nave is a C18 stone font with a baluster stem and octagonal bowl.

767882
ALTRINCHAM, St. George

A large double-aisled brick church constructed in mid C19 in neo-Norm. style with arcades consisting of six bays. The lower section of the w. tower dates from 1799, the original date of building of the first church. The tower stands within the westerly bay of the nave, independent of the arcades which pass by on the n. and s. sides. Evidently, the plan not carried out was to demolish the tower at a later stage in the construction of the new church. There are two painted wooden churchwardens' staves with brass tops and with the Royal monogram "VR" and arms, dated 1838. In the chancel is a wall memorial to the first curate-in-charge, Revd. O. Leicester +1831.

497741
ALVANLEY, St. John Evangelist

The present church in a quiet village dates from 1861 by an unknown artist. A wooden board gives the list of curates since 1677 and vicars since 1861.

773930
ASHTON-ON-MERSEY, St. Martin

The present building was erected in stone in 1714, and the se. tower in 1887 by G. Truefitt. Some old gravestones are attached to the outer wall of the building, the earliest dated 1644. In the churchyard is a C18 sundial with a baluster stem and some ancient stocks with wheels are located in a recess of the boundary wall. The octagonal stone font (late C16) possesses a new stem and base. Also, there is another font, dated 1714, with a small bowl. The church has a volunteer flag presented in 1811, and a copy of the proclamation. Nine benefaction boards form the panels of the front of the w. gallery with dates ranging from 1767 to 1878. There are several wall memorials of C18 and C19.

846616
ASTBURY, St. Mary

The parish church, historically the mother church of Congleton, unquestionably is one of the finest parish churches in Cheshire. Standing above the village green in an unrivalled position, it is distinguished by possessing a semi-detached Dec. nw. tower (c.1366) with parapet spire, and a late C15 Perp. three-storey w. porch. The core of the church was rebuilt in the late medieval period, a fact borne out by the superb C15 Perp. nave and chancel which form a through-church with embattled clerestory overhead. Interestingly, the core is eight feet wider at the w. than the e. end. The windowing of the wall on the n. side of the n. chancel chapel (C13/C14 EE./Dec.) and the n. aisle (C14 Dec.), and

Eastham, decorated tower and spire, c14.

the wall on the s. side of the s. aisle (C14 Dec.) all survive from the previous building. The church which was unscathed by Victorian restorers, contains more late medieval and early Renaissance timberwork than any other church in the county. This includes the particularly ornate late C15 roofs of the nave, chancel and aisles, as well as a handsome ten-bay lierne-vaulted chancel screen (c.1500). The chancel stalls date from the same period. The altar-rails of Dutch strapwork design belong to the late C17 as do the box-pews of the nave and aisles. There is an unusual early C16 wooden lectern consisting of an eagle on a stand. The wooden pulpit is Jacobean and the rare wooden font-cover was made in the same century (C17). There is an altar-tomb in the Moreton chapel in memory of Lady Jane Grey Egerton +1599. Her effigy shows an Elizabethan lady with a ruff. A feature of the churchyard, unique in Cheshire, are a medieval canopied tomb and several worn effigies constructed of sandstone, all dating from C14.

Astbury, late medieval lectern, early C16.

556784
ASTON-BY-SUTTON, St. Peter

The chancel of the small church was built in 1697 and displays Vanbrugh influences. The nave dates from 1736. In the churchyard is a stone font with an octagonal bowl (late C17). There is an unusual wooden tablet on which are painted many coats of arms associated with the Aston family (C18). The holy table (late C17) is by Robert Harper. The church possesses a number of C17, C18 and C19 memorials especially in the chancel to members of the earlier Aston and later Talbot families.

660437
AUDLEM, St. James

The church stands on the edge of high ground where it overlooks the small town of Audlem. The building displays evidence of being substantially remodelled in late C15 when the Perp. style was introduced. Before then, the church had consisted almost entirely of C14 Dec. work, much of which is extant. Thus the nw. tower, n. aisle and chancel belong to the earlier period; while the nave, clerestory and s. aisle date from the later period. The s. porch, also originally constructed in C14, was remodelled a century later too. An uncommon feature of the nave is that both sets of Perp. arcade piers are hexagonal in cross section. The Perp. clerestory overhead is generally agreed to be amongst the best in Cheshire with eight windows on the n. and twelve on the s. side, the windows set closely together. At the w. end of the nave are the original C14 respond of the s. arcade and an equivalent springer of the n. arcade which is located on the se. corner of the tower. In the C14 chancel which was extended by one bay to the e. in C19, the original e. window (c.1400) was re-inserted in the new work. Its tracery is transitional Dec./Perp. The church possesses a C17 wooden pulpit and a two-tier brass chandelier (donated in 1751). In the vicinity of the ground-floor area of the tower are four Randle Holme wooden heraldic tablets (C17 & C18) and a magnificent late C13 parish chest decorated with attractive ironwork.

Chadkirk, redundant church of St. Chad.

Chester Cathedral, free-standing bell tower, 1975.

Audlem nave, part of Perpendicular clerestory, late C15.

398717
BACKFORD, St. Oswald

This small church consists of an early C16 Perp. tower, a late C19 nave and aisles, and a chancel dating from late C13 which displays transitional EE./Dec. characteristics. The latter include a three-light window with intersecting tracery at the e. end and a two-light n. window with Y-tracery. Also in the chancel, coeval with the windows, is a piscina with a trefoil-head and a small aumbry. In the s. aisle, there are six C17 wooden heraldic tablets made by members of the Randle Holme family. These tablets which were carefully restored a few years ago mainly commemorate members of the Morgell and Houghton families.

605503
BADDILEY, St. Michael

The small building is one of the few remaining half-timbered Cheshire churches. Its C14 chancel retains this half-timbered appearance; while its nave is encased in brick (1811). The chancel and nave are separated by a simple wooden medieval screen and tympanum. The latter traverses the whole width of the building and was repainted in post-Restoration days (to display the Royal arms of Charles II, the Mainwaring arms, the Ten Commandments, Lord's Prayer, Creed and sundry biblical texts). The nave is filled with box-pews of c.1700, and in its ne. corner is a three-decker pulpit. In the chancel is a magnificent wall memorial to Sir Thomas Mainwaring +1726.

767524
BARTHOMLEY, St. Bertoline

An obscure Saxon saint provides the dedication of this fine church situated in a small picturesque estate village. Though some of the walling of the s. aisle may date from C12, the building was largely rebuilt in late C15 in the Perp. style. More recently, the chancel was totally rebuilt in 1926 under the patronage of the marquess of Crewe who is buried in the churchyard. The late C15 w. tower is an excellent example of Perp. work in the county. Flanking the twin belfry windows on each of the tower's sides are coats of arms carved in stone of local families. On the n. side of the chancel and only visible externally is a rebuilt Norm. doorway. The Perp. four-bay nave possesses two arcades of which the piers and clerestories overhead are reminiscent of, and may be copies of, those at Nantwich. The handsome panelled roofs of the nave and n. aisle which are of C16 date, are of the camber-beam type. The late C15 n. aisle has windows with elliptical heads and high transoms, features which are good examples of the indigenous Perp. style in Cheshire. At the aisle's e. end is a chapel fenced by a beautiful Perp. wooden screen of early C16 date. The Crewe chapel (s. chancel chapel) was erected c.1528 and conforms to the late

Grappenhall, St. Wilfred.

Wybunbury, perpendicular tower, late c15.

Perp. style. This chapel contains several notable monuments. The latter include effigies of Sir Robert de Foulshurst + c.1390 and Robert Foulshurst, priest, +1529. In addition, there is a table-tomb on which lies an effigy in white marble of Lady Houghton +1887. Designed by Sir J. Edgar Boehm, R.A., it shows her as a serene sleeping figure.

Barthomley north aisle, Perpendicular window with elliptical arch and high transom, late C15.

333839
BEBINGTON, St. Andrew

One of the few churches in Cheshire with a medieval spire (C14 Dec.) which is plain in appearance and of the broach kind. The remaining fabric of the building is of considerable architectural interest owing to the abrupt manner in which the building's reconstruction was terminated at the time of the Suppression c.1540. Thus the e. end of the church was rebuilt in the first half of C16 in a sophisticated late Perp. style. It is equally clear that had the rebuilding not come to a full-stop, it would have proceeded towards the tower. As it happened, the work ceased after the chancel and n. and s. chancel chapels, together with bay 1 of the nave and nave-aisles, had been erected. The design of the C16 archways leading from the chancel into the chancel chapels is particularly attractive. The piers of the chancel arcades are lozenge-shaped with clustered mouldings; while overhead, the whole two areas of walling are finely panelled. The older fabric of the church which was left unchanged, consists of the major portions of the nave (C14 Dec.) and s. aisle (C12 Norm. and late C13

Bebington, St. Andrew.

Bunbury, St. Boniface.

Thurstaston, present church, 1885, sharing the churchyard with tower, 1824, of earlier church.

EE/Dec.), as well as the s. porch (c.1300). The two western bays of the arcade dividing the nave and s. aisle are C12 Norm. These bays include arches which are semi-circular and single-stepped, capitals which are round and decorated with cones separated by reeds, and round piers. The n. aisle, n. arcade and n. porch are C19. The small stone font is C12 Norm, and the wooden parish chest early C16. In the chancel is a set of three stalls with misericords, the remnant of a larger set now dispersed. On the walls of the ground-floor area of the tower are four hatchments commemorating the Green and Mynshall families.

283903
BIDSTON, St. Oswald

The building is one of a number of churches in Cheshire that, apart from the tower, was rebuilt in C19. The tower dates from early C16 and is constructed in the Perp. style. Of special interest in the chancel is a fine and elaborate C19 floor mosaic which has as its main subject an angel together with the inscription, "Holy, holy, holy, Lord God of Sabaoth". The Willis organ (1929) at the west end of the church possesses an attractive organ-case carved with a linenfold pattern and the arms of three families associated with the parish — the Masseys, Stanleys and Viners.

328885
BIRKENHEAD PRIORY, St. Mary & St. James

The priory site which is hemmed in by shipbuilding yards, contains the medieval ruins of the former monastic foundation, together with the partially demolished early C19 church of St. Mary. The C12 Norm, chapter-house which is in good repair, now serves as the modern place of public worship on the site. Its main architectural features are its Norm. quadripartite vault and semi-circular headed windows. In the floor of the sanctuary is an incised stone slab commemorating Thomas Rainford, priest, +1473. Above the chapter-house is a C14 Dec. scriptorium, now used as a meeting-room.

863748
BIRTLES, St. Catherine

Standing in the sole company of the adjacent vicarage, the small church is located in a delightful rural situation. Built of brick in 1840, it possesses a rare octagonal sw. tower, and small transeptal s. porch and matching n. baptistry. Though built fairly recently, the church is filled with ancient carved panelling, mostly Nederlandish of C17, acquired by Thomas Hibbert of Birtles Hall in C19. This panelling includes the w. screen below the organ gallery, work in the baptistry and sanctuary, and sections of the vicar's stall-front and pulpit. The vicar's unusual reading desk is constructed of a C15 (?) lectern in the form of an eagle (or parrot). Hibbert also provided some C16 and C17 stained glass of high quality, the colours having a special richness and brilliance. The C19 chandeliers are believed to be copies of originals in Milan cathedral.

918656
BOSLEY, St. Mary the Virgin

Bosley, St. Mary the Virgin.

Haslington, St. Matthew.

An early C16 Perp. w. tower of red sandstone. The nave was rebuilt in 1777 and a chancel was added in 1834, both being constructed of brick. Of main interest is some modern stained glass, notably the Handel window installed in 1968.

758868
BOWDON, St. Mary the Virgin

This church was totally rebuilt in mid C19. Its chief architectural interest are the roofs of the n. and s. aisles which were preserved in the Victorian reconstruction. Dating from early C16, these roofs are of the camber-beam kind and the beams are elaborately carved and enhanced with complex bosses and coats of arms. There is an imposing C17 monument with a large canopy over a semi-circular arch which commemorates William Brereton +1630, and Jane his wife +1627. Both are displayed in effigy wearing gowns and ruffs. In the s. chancel chapel, there are two big memorials to members of the Booth family: One is in memory of Langham Booth +1724 and Henry Booth +1727; the other is to Henry Booth, Earl of Warrington +1693, and Mary his wife +1690. Both of these memorials were executed by the famous designer André Carpentière. The building also houses the battered stone effigies of two C14 knights, one of which is said to be Sir William Baguley +c.1320.

782648
BRERETON, St. Oswald

Standing in a wooded park, St. Oswald's church has an Elizabethan hall for company. Note the C18 mounting-block at the churchyard gate. The church was one of the few medieval churches in the county to be built in one campaign. Constructed in Perp. style (late C15/early C16), it was untouched by Victorian restorers. The clumsy coupling of chancel roof to nave, and wooden partition between chancel and nave, are possibly the remnant of a former timber-constructed building. The plain w. tower is embraced by n. and s. aisles. The C16 Perp. arcades of the four-bay nave possess substantial piers consisting of four cardinal round shafts separated by four diagonal hollow chamfer mouldings. Above the four arches on each side are six clerestory windows which are set closely together. Each of these windows has an obtusely pointed head and is divided into two uncusped lights. The camber-beam roof of the chancel which dates from C15, is panelled and embellished with carved bosses and crows' feet at the intersections. At the e. end of the chancel is a particularly fine Perp. transomed window with five cusped lights and an obtuse four-centred arch. The highly ornamental altar-rails which are thought by some to be unique in design, belong to C17, as do the altar-table and sanctuary chair. In the sanctuary is an imposing tablet in memory of William Brereton +1618; while in the s. aisle is a large monument commemorating William Smethwick +1643 and Frances Colclough his wife +1632.

Brereton, Mounting-block at entrance to churchyard, C18.

349823
BROMBOROUGH, St. Barnabas

The church was completely rebuilt by Sir G.G. Scott in 1862-64 in a neo-EE. style. The churchyard retains fragments of a Saxon cross.

437605
BRUERA, St. Mary

One of the few Norm. churches in Cheshire. It is a small building of undistinguished external appearance. It possesses a C12 nave and chancel, and a late C15 Perp. s. nave chapel. The nave and chancel are separated by a C12 three-ordered semi-circular archway of which the s. respond is original. The capital of this respond is carved with grotesque faces, foliage and chevron-indentations. In the e. wall of the chancel is a C14 Dec. window with three cusped lights and two reticulation units. The s. nave chapel possesses two large memorials which stand against the s. wall. One of these which shows a putto holding a portrait medallion in front of an obelisk, commemorates Sir Ellis Cunliffe +1767. The other by Nollekens is to Sir Robert Cunliffe +1778 and shows a putto which is seated.

569581
BUNBURY, St. Boniface

One of the great churches of Cheshire both as regards length (160 feet) and general appearance. At first sight it looks Perp., but more careful study reveals much of it to be Dec. The embraced w. tower is the earliest part, dating from early C14 (Dec.). However, its upper section has been substantially reconstructed since the Reformation. The chancel was rebuilt in late C14 when Sir Hugh Calveley +1394 established a collegiate foundation at Bunbury in 1386. The windows of the chancel possess flowing tracery of this period. In the middle of the floor of the chancel is Sir Hugh's altar-tomb. The knight is displayed as a seven-foot long alabaster effigy.

The tomb is surrounded by its original spiked iron railing. To the n. of the chancel is a rare C14 Dec. treasury (now a vestry). The six-bay nave is early C16 Perp. as are the n. and s. aisles. The arcades possess slender piers, each of which has four round cardinal shafts separated by diagonal hollow chamfer mouldings. The clerestory is a Victorian replacement for some small windows inserted above the nave in Elizabethan days. In the centre of the nave is a fine chandelier dated 1756. The n. side of the sanctuary houses an important effigied monument in memory of Sir George Beeston +1601. The Perp. s. chancel chapel was constructed in 1527. It is divided from the chancel by a handsome stone screen which is coeval in date. The octagonal font (1663) retains its original cover. Attached to the e. wall of the n. aisle are the remnants of a C14 stone reredos.

Bunbury, tomb of Sir Hugh Calveley +1394.

317743
BURTON, St. Nicholas

In 1721 the church was substantially rebuilt, the tower and nave surviving from this date. Most of the chancel was reconstructed in C19. However, the n. chancel chapel (EE/Dec.) dates from c.1290 and part of the e. wall of the chancel (Dec.) from early C14. There is a one-handed clock in the tower. Built into one of the walls of the tower is a C13 coffin-lid decorated with a foliated cross with trailing tendrils. The altar-rails (C17) are unusual in that they consist of alternate turned and twisted balusters. There is a rare bible box (C17) in the n. aisle.

Burton neo-Classical nave, 1721.

515565
BURWARDSLEY, St. John

Tucked away in the hills w. of Peckforton, this little church dates from early C17 but was remodelled in 1795. On entering the building, note the round-headed w. window which contains some curious C17? Y-tracery which may not have been originally designed for the actual window. The main interest within the building is a handsome early C19 organ in the nave.

728926
CARRINGTON, St. George

The church in company with the former school building now serving as parish rooms, and the old vicarage, form an oasis in a high density industrial area. The brick building of four bays dates from 1757-59, a shallow apsidal sanctuary being added in 1872. The furniture and fittings all date from C18. They consist of box-pews, pulpit, reading desk, high font with marble bowl and wooden cover, and balustered altar-rails. At the e. end of the nave is a tablet to Revd. John Foster, the first minister, who served for sixty three years in the parish! Above this tablet is a large wooden memorial on which are painted forty eight quarterings of the Booth family. The minister is buried in the se. corner of the churchyard near the entrance to the old vicarage.

940903
CHADKIRK, St. Chad

Now redundant for public worship, this church building consists of a half-timbered chancel which dates from the medieval period. There is also a nave which was constructed in C17. Though stripped of its ecclesiastical contents, the church retains a C18 stone font with a gadrooned round bowl.

857887
CHEADLE, St. Mary

The present building was erected during a long campaign between c.1520 and 1556. Accordingly, apart from minor later additions it was constructed in the late Perp. architectural style. The w. tower may possibly antedate the remainder of the church by a few years. The C16 Perp. s. porch is particularly fine, the date 1634 appearing over the outer doorway indicating repair not initial building. Some of the timberwork of the modern chancel screen may belong to a late medieval rood-screen. At the e. ends of the side-aisles are two ancient wooden screens. That on the n. side (c.1529) fences the Savage chapel; while that on the s. side (of similar date) fences the Brereton or Honford chapel. This second screen which is not as elaborate in design as the Savage screen, possesses on its upper rail facing the nave carvings of tuns entwined with briar leaves and branches, the rebus on the name of the founder of the chapel, Sir Urian Brereton. The s. chapel houses two altar-tombs on one of which are the alabaster effigies of two late C15 or early C16 knights, probably Sir John Stanley and William Honford). On the other tomb, there is an effigy of Sir Thomas Brereton +1673.

406665
CHESTER,
Cathedral of Christ & The Blessed Virgin Mary

Compared with many other medieval cathedrals in England, the cathedral may not be particularly large or impressive. For one reason, it is considerably asymmetrical owing to the difference in size of the n. and s. transepts. The explanation for this is that the monastic buildings which are still very extensive, have always hemmed in the cathedral closely on the n. side and thus have prevented the expansion of the small transept on that side. The church has been rebuilt in part several times since the coming of the Normans and therefore displays several architectural styles in its fabric. Norm. work of C12 survives in the nw. tower (now the baptistry), n. aisle and n. transept. The EE. lady chapel dates from late C13 and the Dec. choir from early C14. Later still are the s. transept, s. side of the nave and the s. aisle (all mid C14 Dec.). The final phase of medieval construction includes the n. side of the nave, nave clerestory, central tower, s. porch, sw. tower (now the consistory court) and w. front (all late C15 & early C16 Perp.). Apart from major restorations carried out in C19, the remaining construction of note is the detached bell tower designed by George Pace, and opened in 1975. The font installed in 1885 has a rectangular bowl, spindly legs and is covered with Christian symbols. Though ancient in appearance, it may not be older than C19. The n. archway leading from the interstitium to the n. transept frames the organ-loft and case (1876) designed by Sir G. Gilbert Scott and generally reckoned to be a magnificent piece of work. The finest artefact of the cathedral are the choir stalls (c.1385). With their spiky canopies embellished with crocketed arches and nearly fifty misericords, they are the single outstanding feature of the cathedral and are among the best in the land. At the w. end of the lady chapel is the restored stone shrine (mid C14) of St. Werburgh, re-assembled from fragments. Of the monastic buildings much Norm. fabric of early C12 remains (especially the undercroft, cloister and abbot's chapel). The C13 EE. vestibule which forms the entrance to the chapter-house, has vaulting supported on slender columns. However, these columns do not possess capitals, a characteristic unusual for the period. The chapter-house (C13 EE.) is rectangular in plan with sets of slender lancet windows. In the refectory which originally dates from C12 Norm. period, is the well-preserved stone reading pulpit (c.1290).

405658
CHESTER, Chapel of St. Mary de Castro

The small late C12 or early C13 EE. chapel forms the first floor of the three-stage Agricola (Caesar's) Tower of Chester Castle. The ground-floor of the tower forms a crypt which was restored in early C14 by Richard the Engineer. He is credited with inserting the stone sexpartite vault in this crypt. The chapel above consists of two bays and has a quadripartite vault. The mouldings of the ribs of this vault which consist of filleted triple-rolls, as well as the mouldings of the responds from which the ribs spring, are among the best EE. work in the county.

409661
CHESTER, St. John Baptist

Architecturally, this is perhaps the most interesting church in Cheshire. Built by the Normans at the end of C11 as a great cruciform cathedral (in which capacity it served for just twenty years), much of its fabric was allowed to fall into ruin in C16. But for its conversion from collegiate to parish church by local townspeople during the reign of Elizabeth I, it would have been totally destroyed. Though shorn of its former glory, it is still a noble building. The surviving original fabric (late C11 & most of C12 Norm.) includes the four-bay nave, n. and s. aisles, interstitium, and sections of the transepts and former choir. At the w. end is the stump of the massive nw. tower which possesses a C12 Norm. core; while at the e. end are the remains of the choir chapels (C12 Norm. & C14 Dec.). On the s. side of the church is the semi-derelict chapter-house (C14 Dec.). The ne. tower which is not really in keeping with the rest of the building, dates from C19. The massive late C11 Norm. piers of the nave are plain and round, and their capitals which are also round, are scalloped. Overhead, the arches are semi-circular and double-stepped. The triforium dates from c.1190, displaying a transitional Norm/EE. style. The nave clerestory is mature EE. of mid C13 date, with capitals having richly carved foliage. The Norm. interstitium (c.1100), an impressive piece of work, comprises four large semi-circular arches arranged in a square with massive corner piers. Like the nave arches, these arches are double-stepped. In the present lady chapel is a large marble memorial by Edward Pearce which commemorates Diana Warburton +1693. This memorial displays a cloth-covered erect skeleton. The church has a collection of nine Randle Holme wooden heraldic tablets belonging to C17.

406658
CHESTER, St. Mary on the Hill

Redundant as a church, it now forms an education centre. Externally, the building which displays signs of having been drastically restored in C19, resembles the type of church prevalent in the western part of the county. Most of it was reconstructed in the late C15/early C16 in the Perp. style. However, the s. chancel (Troutbeck) chapel was rebuilt in 1693. The only remnants antedating the Perp. rebuild are the C14 Dec. chancel arch and tower arch. The C19 n. porch protects a handsome C16 Perp. inner doorway which has a Tudor arch set within a square frame moulded with quatrefoils etc. The glory of the church is the C16 camber-beam nave roof, its three bays each being divided into forty panels. In the middle of the central bay of this roof, there are five bosses inscribed with the letters M A R I A in Old English block capitals. Though the church's furniture has been removed, there are still a number of ancient monuments to see. Thus in the n. chancel chapel are two free-standing tombs, one of which belongs to Thomas Gamul, recorder of Chester, +1613. The second commemorates Philip Oldfield +1616. Both tombs are effigied in the style of the period. The n. aisle is the resting place of four generations of the Randle Holme family who are commemorated by two wall-memorials.

406662
CHESTER, St. Michael

Another redundant Chester church now used as a heritage centre. Extensively rebuilt internally as well as externally in C19, it retains a C14 Dec. arcade which separates the nave (mainly C19) from the n. aisle (also mainly C19). The octagonal capitals of the piers of this arcade have a quatrefoil shaped fleuron on each of the eight facets. The other feature of special interest is the chancel roof. Constructed in 1496, it is of the arch-braced type and was widened on the s. side in 1678 when the chancel was enlarged.

Chester, St. Michael.

406659
CHESTER, St. Olave

A small redundant church now used as an annex by the local college of further education. The former church is a small rectangular building of uncertain pre-Reformation date. However, the e. end appears to have been made longer towards the end of the medieval period.

404663
CHESTER, St. Peter

The church stands at the centre of the city where four of the main streets meet. It is believed to have been erected on the site of the s. side of the Roman Praetorium and to contain traces of Roman masonry in its fabric. Possessing an unusually broad plan owing to the need to conserve space in this part of the city, the building consists of a Dec. w. tower that has been restored many times since it was first constructed in C14, a Perp. combined nave and chancel of two bays (C15), n. and s. aisles (C15 Perp.), and a Perp. outer n. aisle constructed in C16. The tower which is embraced, contains — rarely for Cheshire — a C15 stone-vaulted ceiling at first floor level. On the ne. pier under the tower is an ogee-canopied niche which originally housed a carved stone figure of the Virgin and Child. The niche is surrounded by a well-preserved medieval wall painting, "The coming of the Magi to the Stable at Bethlehem". Under the gallery of the s. aisle are three corbel-heads of medieval origin of which the subjects are an angel, a woman and an old man. Nearby is the monumental brass of a man wearing the robes of a lawyer (c.1460). The inner n. aisle possesses a much-restored camber-beam roof of C15 with gilded bosses. On the n. wall of the church, there are two C17 Randle Holme wooden heraldic tablets.

441658
CHRISTLETON, St. James

This is yet another Cheshire church which has been completely rebuilt, that is save for the lower part of the C15 Perp. w. tower. The main part of the church is the work (1875-77) of W. Butterfield. On the upper part of the tower facing the road is a handsome clockface dated 1868.

822558
CHURCH LAWTON, All Saints

Sited on what appears to be an artificial mound close to Lawton hall, the church dates from Norm. times. However, the only part of the building surviving from this period is the C12 s. doorway. The latter possesses a chevron-moulded semi-circular arch below which are scalloped capitals. The austere Perp. w. tower constructed of large blocks of sandstone dates from C16. It was erected by John Bybber, rector 1530-55, whose initials appear in Lombardic letters separated by the outline of a chalice on the s. face of the tower. Within the base of the tower, there is a recessed altar-tomb to Bybber under a plain four-centred arch. The remainder of the church, constructed in brick, was rebuilt in 1803. On the gallery front at the w. end of the nave hangs a frame of canvas on which are painted the Royal arms of George III. Underneath the gallery, displayed on the s. wall, are some C13 flooring tiles discovered during restoration in 1874. There are six well-preserved hatchments of the Lawton family hanging round the walls of the nave.

Church Lawton nave, Norman south doorway, C12.

666607
CHURCH MINSHULL, St. Bartholomew

A brick-built church with stone dressings located in an unspoilt black-and-white village in the Weaver valley. The w. tower dates from 1702 and the body of the church from 1704. The former date is picked out in dark brick on the wall on either side of the s. clockface. According to a local tradition, the round piers of the nave are medieval, the sole surviving part of the fabric belonging to an earlier half-timbered building. Many members of the Cholmondeley family of Vale Royal are buried in a vault underneath the n. aisle, and their names are recorded on a big tablet covering the period, 1666-1815, which is placed on the e. wall of this aisle. The church contains a Randle Holme wooden heraldic tablet in memory of Jane Cholmondeley +1666. The gadrooned font dates from 1717.

453553
CODDINGTON, St. Mary

The present building is by J. Atkinson (1833). There is a sundial on an octagonal stem and square base (1795). Several items of antiquarian interest inside the church include a brass listing members of the Massie of Coddington family interred in a vault (1610-1802), a pulpit and reading desk constructed of old wooden panels decorated with linenfold carving (C17), three-sided altar-rails (Laudian) with Aldersey arms carved in quatrefoils (C17), a C17 parish chest with three locks, and a hatchment of the Alderseys.

859628
CONGLETON, St. Peter

Though externally unprepossessing, this church is a fine example of C18 interior design. The main part of the building was rebuilt in 1742 in neo-Classical style; while in 1786 the w. tower was given a Gothick casing around its medieval core. The inside of the five-bay nave which is continuous with the one-bay chancel presents a pleasing and dignified appearance with Palladian proportions and symmetry. The whole forms a preaching house with, unusually, a C17 pulpit set in the middle of the nave at its e. end. On either side of e. window are paintings of St. Peter and St. Paul, by E. Penny of Knutsford (1748). Items of interest in the s. aisle are the Royal arms of William III (1702) and a medieval timber chest. The most imposing memorial in the church is to Col. Sir Thomas Reade +1849. Attached to the e. wall of the s. chapel, it displays in semi-relief a slave kneeling in prayer by a palm tree, a reminder of Sir Thomas's action while British Consul General at Tunis of pursuading the Bey of that country to abolish slavery.

702566
COPPENHALL, St. Michael

The chancel dates from 1883-86 by J. Brooks and the nave from 1907-10 by J. Brooks, Son & Adkins, all in red brick. Little survives from earlier buildings on the site save a C17 wooden timber chest with three locks, a wooden bench (c.1823) and two mid C19 wall tablets.

581828
DARESBURY, All Saints

The village was the birthplace of Lewis Carroll (or more properly Revd. C.L. Dodgson) the author of "Alice in Wonderland". He is remembered in the stained glass of a five-light window in the Daniell or s. chancel chapel. The glass designed by Geoffrey Webb and dedicated in 1934 features the "Adoration of the Babe of Bethlehem" and shows some of the Alice characters. The Perp. w. tower dates from mid C16, and the remainder of the church from 1870-72 when it was rebuilt by Paley & Austin. It is believed that the date 1110 which is carved on the s. face of the tower is erroneous, due to C17 restorers mistakenly copying the original date 1550. A board (dated 1730) on the wall of the ringing chamber has painted on it rhyming rules for bellringers which include the acrostic

D-A-R-E-S-B-U-R-Y. In the chancel are thirty four Perp. wooden panels of the former rood-screen. Dating from C16, they display some fine perforated tracery in eleven modes of treatment with one panel showing the Green Man. In the floor of the chancel, there is a handsome C19 brass to the memory of General Peter Heron +1848*. There is in the nave a C17 wooden pulpit with panels that are intricately carved.

---

*The brass erroneously gives the date of death of General Heron as MDCCCIV (1804).

663713
DAVENHAM, St. Wilfrid

The whole of the earlier church was replaced by the present building during 1844-70. A wall tablet under the tower arch commemorates William Tomkinson +1770. Other wall memorials are of C18 and C19.

560686
DELAMERE, St. Peter

The small stone church is located in an isolated rural situation on a gently sloping hillside. The building which includes a neat w. tower, was constructed by J. Gunnery in 1816-17.

975845
DISLEY, St. Mary

The church crowns a hillside above the small town of Disley. It was first constructed c.1510-58. Its Perp. w. tower — a rather inelegant structure — and w. porch survive from this period. The remainder was built in 1824-35, though the late medieval nave roof was retained. This roof unquestionably is the best feature of the church. Consisting of the camber-beam type, it extends to six bays and is divided into many panels, being decorated with demi-angels, elaborately carved bosses and crows' feet. Taken as a whole, it is probably the most highly decorated roof in the county. A stone in the central aisle of the nave marks the grave of Joseph Watson +1753. He was the legendary deer keeper at Lyme park, living to the ripe old age of 104. The church possesses a collection of medieval glass, including some in the e. window of the chancel (dated 1535) believed to have come from Nuremburg. On the parapet of the w. gallery are the Royal arms of George IV (c.1820). The s. aisle includes a small chapel at its e. end in which is a bible box (1693).

Disley nave, roof detail, C16.

362609
DODLESTON, St. Mary

Historically, the church and village of Dodleston came into being when Dodleston castle was constructed to help protect the city of Chester on the latter's w. side. The church which is located close to the moat of the castle, was largely rebuilt in 1869-70 by J. Douglas. However, the lower part of the C16 Perp. w. tower remains from the medieval period. On the exterior of the n. wall of the tower are pitted marks said to have been made by muskets fired during the Civil War. At the w. end of the nave are the remains of a C13 foliated coffin-lid; and there is a benefaction board (1803) nearby. The C16 Perp. tower arch which has a continuous double-chamfered moulding, is surmounted by the Royal arms of Charles II (1660). Several ancient memorials are situated in the ground-floor area of the tower. Chief of these is a black marble slab in which is set a lozenge of white marble. This memorial displays a Latin inscription to the erstwhile Lord Chancellor of England, Sir Thomas Egerton +1617.

361800
EASTHAM. St. Mary the Blessed Virgin

The church is located in the middle of the village of Eastham on a raised triangular-shaped churchyard which possesses a yew tree that may by fifteen hundred years old. The church has been restored many times in its long history, the most drastic in the period 1876-80 when David Walker reroofed the nave and aisles, and lowered some of the floors. The oldest part of the building is the C12 n. wall of the n. chancel chapel, most of which is C15 Perp. Other sections of St. Mary's belong to a variety of periods — the nave is mainly C13 EE., the tower C14 Dec., the n. and s. aisles C15 Perp., the s. porch C16 Perp., and the chancel C19. The w. tower is one of the few medieval towers in Cheshire to possess a spire (re-assembled in 1751), the latter of the broach kind with four added pinnacles. The ground-floor area of the tower is used as a baptistry and it contains a plain circular C12 Norm. font. The arcades of the four-bay nave are C13 EE., the n. being slightly older that the s. On one of the detached capitals of the n. side is some nailhead ornamentation. At the e. end of the s. aisle is a late C16 oaken parish chest that must be all of nine feet long. Nearby, is a C17 wooden collecting box with a long handle. The Hooton or Stanley chapel (n. chancel chapel) contains two important altar-tombs: One, constructed of alabaster, has six crude columns and is in memory of Charlotte Lady Stanley +1662; the other commemorates Sir William Stanley +1612. It is made of sandstone, with tapering pilasters and simple geometrical embellishments. In the n. aisle is a large display of the Royal arms of George III (1772) and a benefaction board (1709).

413626
ECCLESTON, St. Mary the Virgin

A fragment of the previous church by W. Porden, 1809-13, is in the old churchyard where the dukes of Westminster are interred. The handsome present building was designed by G.F. Bodley (1899). The gate pillars and elegant wrought-iron gates at the main entrance are C18 and there is a sundial with baluster stem (1732). Inside the church is a wooden tablet to Sir Richard Grosvenor (1624) and a benefaction board (1718-48). Also, there is a modern brass plaque identifying those members of the Grosvenor family, 1599-1894, buried in the old churchyard.

413545
FARNDON, St. Chad

A church which stands above the e. bank of the River Dee facing its Welsh partner on the other side, St. Chad's church at Holt. Only the lower part of the w. tower (C14 Dec.) retains its medieval fabric. The rest of the building was rebuilt in 1658 following serious damage caused in the Civil War. In the n. aisle is the worn effigy of a knight said to be Patrick de Barton c.1340. The Barnston or s. aisle chapel contains numerous wall-memorials to members of that family. Of these, two are Randle Holme wooden heraldic tablets which commemorate John Barnston +1661, and William Barnston +1664. The e. window of the chapel has some noteworthy stained glass showing figures and scenes from the Civil War period, the glass being restored in 1894. On the n. side of the churchyard is a sundial (1793) with a big baluster-shaped stem.

521773
FRODSHAM, St. Lawrence

This is, historically speaking, an important Cheshire church since it retains substantial late C12 Norm. work in the nave. Much of the remainder of the building belongs to C14 and C15. But there was a major restoration in 1880-82 when Bodley & Garner rebuilt the s. aisle and reconstructed the e. end of the nave. The C14 Dec. w. tower is plain in appearance and has been rebuilt at its summit (C19). There are two C18 porches, the s. constructed in 1715 and the n. in 1724. The nave is mainly C12 Norm. with, unusually for Cheshire, a Norm. clerestory. The arches of the two w. bays are original, but those of the next bay (i.e. to the e.) were built (or rebuilt) by Bodley & Garner. The Norm. piers of c.1170 are cylindrical in shape except for the free-standing nw. pier which is octagonal and slightly later in date (c.1200). The piers have capitals with square abaci; while the capitals themselves are carved with shallow acanthus foliage on their sides, and curly volutes on the

Frodsham, St. Lawrence.

corners. The Norm. clerestory possesses three deeply-splayed semi-circular windows on each side. In the internal n. and s. walls of the tower are two ancient blocked arches, the original purpose of which remains obscure. Also, set into the s. wall of the tower are some fragments of carved stone including a Saxon carving of "Christ in Glory". The chancel arch is C14 Dec. as is the w. section of the chancel. Its C15 Perp. e. window of seven lights is among the best of its type in the county. There is a C15 Perp. sedile under a canopy and an unusual piscina of the same period with a carved head. The altar-rails (c.1700) have twisted balusters. The n. aisle is C14 Dec. and it contains two original windows with some flowing tracery. In the C15 Perp. Helsby or n. chancel chapel is an altar-table (1678) of somewhat curious design made by Robert Harper, behind which is a C17 reredos. In the Kingsley or s. chancel chapel is a Jacobean altar-table.

890697
GAWSWORTH, St. James

A handsome Perp. church in a pretty village, it dates almost in its entirety from the second half of C15. Thus the wide aisleless nave was commenced c.1430, and the tower and chancel forty or fifty years later. The whole church was completed c.1500. The fine tall w. tower which is Perp., has fifteen carved shields dispersed around its sides displaying the arms of ancient Cheshire families. The C15 Perp. nave is of three bays. It has an uncommon C15 rafter-beam roof which displays traces of its former medieval colouring. There is a C15 font with a large octagonal bowl. The chancel screen (1894) by J. Oldrid Scott is said to be a copy of that at Elvaston, Derbs. The C15 roof of the chancel which is finer than that of the nave, is of the camber-beam type and is divided into panels. The main focus of interest in the chancel is the group of four Fitton memorials which are all located in the sanctuary. The oldest is a table-tomb commemorating Francis Fitton +1608. His effigy lies on the table and underneath is a headless skeleton in a shroud. A second is the table-tomb of Sir Edward Fitton +1619. He is shown with his wife in effigy. The third tomb shows Dame Alice Fitton +1627, seated in widow's garb with her children. A fourth commemorates Sir Edward Fitton +1643, also in effigy on a table-tomb with his wife.

779700
GOOSTREY, St. Luke

The church is a rebuild of 1792-96 in brick. The churchyard contains a sundial with baluster stem (1798). There is a handsome C15 stone font with quatrefoils on an octagonal bowl, and shields within panelled faces on an octagonal stem. The Royal arms (c.1800) are of George III, and there are a sanctuary chair (C17) and wooden chest (C18). Probably the oldest memorial is a ledger-stone to Mary Worthington +1661. Several C18 and C19 memorials mark members of the Booth and Glegg families.

Goostrey, Perpendicular font, C15.

639863
GRAPPENHALL, St. Wilfrid

Though close to industrialised Warrington, the church is located in a pleasant environment at the end of a cobbled village street. The building devoid of pinnacles and battlements save on the tower, conforms to the e. Cheshire style with gabled roofs and overhanging eaves. The oldest portion of the church is a fragment of the nave which is C12 Norm, and next comes the C14 Dec. s. chancel chapel. Most of the remainder dates from C16 and is Perp. in style. Paley & Austin undertook a big restoration in 1874 when they rebuilt the n. chancel transept. The C16 Perp. w. tower which looks rather austere, possesses on its w. side the carved figure of a grinning animal said to be the original Cheshire Cat. The nave and chancel are continuous with five bays to the nave and two to the chancel. The nave was largely restored in C16, the date 1539 appearing on a s. pier near the w. end. Above the arches of the s. arcade is a C12 Norm. corbel-table which runs the whole length of the five bays of the nave. The font which is rectangular and embellished with blind arcading, is also C12 Norm. Near it is a large fragment of C15 stained glass on which appears the Virgin Mary. In the C16 Perp. chancel, there is a well-preserved effigy of Sir William Boydell +1275. The C19 reredos of which the subject is "The Last Supper", is carved of wood in semi-relief. The window tracery of the C14 Dec. e. window in the Boydell or s. chancel chapel contains some of the best surviving stained glass of medieval date in the county. Of the same age as the window, the glass shows an array of saints. On the n. side of the church are the Royal arms of Queen Anne (1704). There are two wooden chests one C13 and the other C18, the latter having elaborate carvings.

469684
GREAT BARROW, St. Bartholomew

The round churchyard and name of the parish denote a place of considerable antiquity. However, nothing belonging to the church or its environs survives earlier than from the late medieval period. Near the s. porch is a sundial (1705) with an octagonal stem. The oldest part of the building is the arcade (early C16 Perp.) which divides the nave from the early C17 n. aisle. The Tudor arches of this arcade are flattened and four-centred with points that have almost disappeared. The chancel, rebuilt by Dr. Bridgman of Chester, dates from 1671; and the w. tower was constructed in 1744 in neo-Classical style. J. Douglas restored the nave and built the s. porch in 1883. The roof of the chancel, portions of which may date from C17, is of the arch-brace and hammerbeam type. It displays the arms of Dr. Bridgman. There are several benefaction boards (1711, 1725 and 1848) on the walls of the ground-floor area of the tower; while close by is a parish chest (1718). The plain octagonal font (1713) does not have a classical appearance.

Great Barrow, neo-Classical tower, 1744.

664775
GREAT BUDWORTH, St. Mary and All Saints

One of the great parish churches of Cheshire, it is set on a ridge above two meres and is at the centre of a picture-book village. It is constructed of large blocks of sandstone, some of which are worn excessively. The present building dates from C14, although much of it was reconstructed in C15 and C16. The early C16 Perp. w. tower was built by Thomas Hunter who was also responsible for the later tower at Witton. The six-bay nave dates from C14 on the n. side, and C15 on the s., with Dec. and Perp. arches on each side respectively. The clerestory is C16 Perp. and the wall space between it and the arcades is panelled with small stone ribs. High up in the ne. corner of the nave can be seen the entrance to the former rood-loft. An unusual feature are the two blocked windows (compare Cotswold churches) above the chancel arch. The nave roof is early C16 and of the camber-beam kind. There is a fine C15 font with octagonal bowl, quatrefoils and carved heads. In the nave floor is a handsome Victorian memorial brass to Joseph Leigh +1840. The chancel which has a C14 core, was remodelled in the

Great Budworth south aisle, part of Perpendicular embattled parapet displaying a continuous moulding, late C15/early C16.

Perp. style a century later notably through the insertion of fine arcades on either side and a five-light e. window. The s. side of the church is entirely Perp. dating from C15 and C16. This includes the s. chancel chapel in which there is a large monument to the memory of Sir Peter Warburton +1813; while in the s. aisle are mounted eight staves (c.1830) for churchwardens and sidesmen. Nearby on the wall is a benefaction board (1703). In the s. aisle chapel is a badly damaged alabaster effigy of Sir John Warburton +1575. Also here are five C13 oak stalls, probably the oldest examples of such furniture in Cheshire. The n. aisle and n. aisle chapel or transept are C14 Dec., and the n. chancel chapel is C16 Perp.

449682
GUILDEN SUTTON, St. John Baptist

A rebuild in brick of 1815, the small church possesses a wooden panelled archway to the w. door inscribed 1698. There is a remnant of a wooden half-screen carved with the name Henry Bunbury and the date 1527. The stone font with plain round bowl is dated 1635. Twisted baluster altar-rails (C18) are repositioned in front of the chancel screen. Also, there is a Randle Holme wooden heraldic tablet to Robert Whitehead +1693.

466579
HANDLEY, All Saints

A small building largely rebuilt in Victorian days. The Perp. w. tower which is dated 1512 on its w. face, is the oldest surviving part. It is a pleasing structure with some nicely decorated stonework, especially the canopied and finialed w. window. In 1854 James Harrison rebuilt the rest of the church, at the same time sparing the nave roof of 1661. The latter is largely original with hammerbeams, arch-braces and collar-beams. On the wall by the s. door is a handsome cartouche in memory of John Edge +1684. Also, there is a small plain C17 font and a wooden parish chest (1677). In the ground-floor area of the tower is a benefaction board (dated 1719 and copied 1852) and another board in poor condition displaying the Royal arms (of uncertain date).

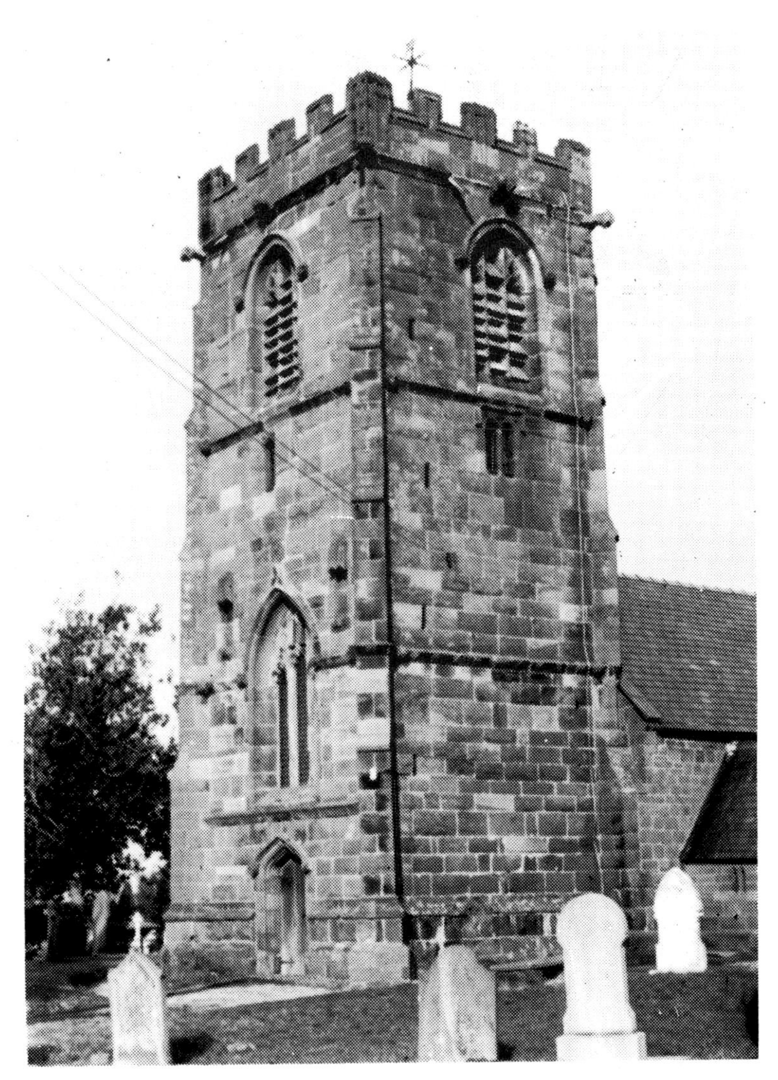

Handley, Perpendicular tower, 1512.

485622
HARGRAVE, St. Peter

This little church was built in 1627 at the instigation of Thomas Moulson, a local boy who became lord mayor of London. The building constructed of red sandstone is rectangular and consists of a five-bay nave-cum-chancel. The roof is largely original comprising a hammerbeam and arch-brace type of construction. There is an impressive reredos presented to the church in 1898 by the duke of Westminster. This has as its centre-piece the picture "Christ in Glory" which is topped by a triple-arched canopy.

500553
HARTHILL, All Saints

The small church clings to a ridge forming part of the Broxton hills. It consists of a nave and chancel which date from 1609 when the medieval church was rebuilt. The nave and chancel of five bays are continuous but divided by a tall timber chancel screen inscribed with the date 1609. On the e. side of this screen appear the names and heraldic arms of incumbents of the parish; on the w. side are those of the lords of the manor. The roof, too, is dated 1609 but it was substantially restored in C19. It is arch-braced with hammerbeams carried on stone corbels, with supporting brackets which are richly carved. The church possesses two benefaction boards of 1707 and 1733.

737560
HASLINGTON, St. Matthew

The w. section of the church was constructed in 1810, and the e. end in 1909 by R.T. Longden.

266812
HESWALL, St. Peter

Looking out over the Dee estuary, the church was completely rebuilt by J. Francis Doyle in 1879, with the exception of the sw. tower. The chancel was extended and the Brocklebank or s. chancel chapel built in 1893, also by Doyle. The plain but well-proportioned tower is late C14 in its lower stage and C16 in its upper stage including its Perp. belfry windows. The ground-floor area of the tower is a repository for the ancient wall memorials of the church which were brought here after the Victorian restoration. These include a small white alabaster plaque on which is carved the seal of William de Hesele Wele who lived in early C14. In addition, there are a black marble tablet on which has been incised the civilian figure of John Glegg +1619, and a tablet of white and grey marble under an open pediment in memory of Katherine Glegg +1666. The church possesses three fonts of the following dates: C17, 1739 and C19. On a small board are the Royal arms of George III. The Brocklebank chapel is designed in a richer neo-Gothic style than the remainder of the church, and is separated from the chancel by a handsome C19 stone screen.

762673
HOLMES CHAPEL, St. Luke

The church of St. Luke is situated in an island churchyard in the centre of the recently enlarged village. The Perp. w. tower which is late C15, is plain in appearance. The body of the church is not what it seems from outside. Actually it has a complex timber-framed construction dating from early C15. About the year 1700 the w. end of the chancel and side-aisles were encased in brick, and soon afterwards (c.1732) the chancel was lengthened. The gallery which was erected in 1705, runs round two sides of the nave only — the s. and w. sides. The fine and original nave roof which dates from early C15, survives because until recently it was hidden under a later plaster ceiling. Below this roof and supporting it, there are two timber arcades with octagonal piers belonging to the same medieval period. Hanging from the nave roof is a two-tier brass chandelier (1708), possibly the oldest in the county.

412541
HOLT, St. Chad

The church stands on the w. bank of the River Dee immediately opposite the church at Farndon. From outside it looks like a big Perp. building, and indeed the four-light windows divided by deep buttresses running the full length of the aisles and chancel chapels on n. and s. sides as well as the fine e. facade indicate that a major reconstruction occurred in late C15. On the s. side of the church is a handsome late C15 Perp. doorway on one of the spandrels of which are the arms of Henry VIII. It is likely that the building never received an intended nave and chancel clerestory. The tower is C14 Dec. except for its w. window of three lights (C15 Perp.). Inside, the church displays an earlier history: The narrow EE. nave of c.1250 possesses two five-bay arcades with acutely pointed arches. The C15 two-bay chancel is the product of the late Perp. remodelling when the chancel arch was removed and new arcading introduced to match the alignment of the arcades of the nave. The camber-beam roof of the chancel which is ornately decorated with quatrefoils over the sanctuary, dates from late C15

Holt south aisle, label of Perpendicular doorway, late C15.

or early C16 and is panelled. The C15 font is particularly beautiful, being lavishly covered with carving, supported by shields and badges outlining the history of the manor and its various owners. On the n. wall of the n. chancel chapel is a small rectangular brass tablet (dated 1666) which possesses an acrostic verse by Sylvanus Crue to his deceased relative Thomas Crue.

450764
INCE, St. James

On the opposite side of the road from a giant petro-chemical plant, the small church stands in an oasis of mature trees. It possesses a C14 Dec. chancel and a late C15 Perp. tower which uncommonly does not have a great w. window or w. doorway. The remainder of the church which is of the two-aisled type, was rebuilt by E. Hodkinson in 1854. Architecturally, the chancel is the most important part of the building. In its e. wall is a Dec. three-light window. Its arch-braced roof though much restored, dates from 1671. On its n. wall are four brass memorial plates with dates of 1701, 1706 twice, and 1708. Nearby, there is a handsome wall memorial to Edmund Waldegrave Park Yates +1896. The chancel also has some late C17 altar-rails with delicately twisted balusters and a two-tier chandelier (1724). In the nave are the Royal arms of Queen Anne.

753785
KNUTSFORD, St. John Baptist

This large town church was built by J. Garlive in 1741-44, and the chancel was rebuilt and enlarged in 1879. The nave comprises four bays with two arcades constructed of Tuscan pillars. In the nave is a fine two-tier chandelier of 1763. There are two fonts, one coeval with the C18 building of the church, and the second (1865) out of keeping with the general style. Two wooden churchwardens' staves bear the inscriptions "VR 1846 Knutsford". In the gallery of the n. aisle is a C18 hatchment of the Legh family, and in the s. aisle a wall memorial by R. Westmacott to Elizabeth Legh +1823. The walls of the ground-floor area of the w. tower which serves as a porch, are lined with benefaction boards possessing the following dates: 1683, 1718, 1719, 1830, 1838 and 1848. Nearby on a small board are painted the Royal arms described as being of the second year of the reign of William IV. Also, there is a Randle Holme heraldic tablet to John Legh +1660.

Knutsford St. John Baptist, neo-Classical tower, 1744.

599654
LITTLE BUDWORTH, St. Peter

The small church is situated on a bank in the middle of the pretty village. The churchyard has a good collection of C18 and C19 table-tombs. The Perp. w. tower was built between 1490 and 1526. The remainder of the building, however, dates from 1800, the product of a gift of £1,000 made by Ralph Kirkham a Manchester merchant. The tower possesses an old clock (1728) with a clock face on the s. side dated 1785. The four-bay nave is a poor example of the neo-Classical style. On the e. wall above the Egerton family pew and vault is a large picture by an unknown artist of C17, "The Deposition from the Cross". Two fittings of interest are a C18 painted font with gadrooned bowl and a Georgian pulpit (c.1800).

615759
LITTLE LEIGH, St. Michael

The existing building is by E. Kirby, dating from 1878-79.

743742
LOWER PEOVER, St. Oswald

In an attractive village approached via a cobbled lane, the church is one of the best remaining half-timbered churches in the county. The main part of the building dates from C14, though the e. chapels are later (C17). The Perp. w. tower which is made of Alderley sandstone, is late C16. A Salvin carried out major repairs in 1852 when he replaced the single span roof over the nave and side-aisles by three gabled roofs. Internally, the church is full of interest as it contains many fittings and fixtures of C17. The C14 nave has four bays with timber arcades leading to the aisles. The nave and aisles are filled with C17 box-pews. There is an attractive C17 wooden pulpit with delightful inlaid work. Other timbered products of the same period include the half-screen between nave and chancel, lectern, altar-rails, choir stall fronts, and holy table. The C14 or C15 plain font has a Jacobean cover; while attached to one of the n. piers are some wooden breadshelves (1720 and 1739). The lower part of the timber screen of the Holford or n. chancel chapel may be medieval, although it carries the date of the chapel, 1624, on its top-rail. The s. chancel chapel (c.1610) consists of two parts of which the e. is the small Shakerley mortuary chapel, divided from the w. section by a heavy Jacobean screen. The e. chapel possesses four monuments to members of the Shakerley family of which the most imposing is that to Sir Geoffrey Shakerley +1696. The w. section contains a wooden hand thought to represent the hand of St. Oswald, and a huge wooden dugout chest (C13).

Lower Peover, St. Oswald.

614789
LOWER WHITLEY, St. Luke

Another small church standing just off the main road between Weaverham and Warrington. Curiously, the timber lichgate, a memorial to men who fell in the 1914-18 War, houses the church clock. The building is a small brick edifice which was originally constructed in early C17. This was followed by restorations in 1864 and 1880. The C17 nave is distinguished by a fine roof (1620) which is of hammerbeam and arch-brace construction and which possesses highly decorated Jacobean brackets and small turned pendants. The w. section of the C17 two-part chancel has a roof of similar date and appearance.

Lower Whitley lichgate and clock of C20, in front of church.

694872
LYMM, St. Mary

The church stands on a bank high above the small town of Lymm. The main part of the church was rebuilt by J. Dobson in 1850-52 and the tower by J.S. Crowther in 1888-90. Externally, the church retains a C18 sundial with a stone baluster stem. Internally, in the s. wall is a rebuilt medieval canopied tomb containing a so-called Roman altar. A wooden pulpit possesses the date 1623, and there is a C17 octagonal font. Besides one or two later wall monuments, there is a wooden memorial to William Domvylle +1686. Other items of interest include some C18 hatchments and two early C19 churchwardens' staves.

914736
MACCLESFIELD, Christ Church

A big gaunt church, now redundant, constructed of brick with stone quoins, dating from 1775-76. It has a high w. tower of four stages, a nave of seven bays and a shallow chancel. Inside, there is a continuous gallery which runs round three sides of the nave. The fittings and furniture all date from the Georgian period. These include the high panelled wooden pulpit which is reached by a long flight of steps. The chief monument in the church is that of the founder of the building, Charles Roe +1781. This memorial is by Bacon and it includes a medallion displaying Roe's portrait.

974722
MACCLESFIELD,
Forest Chapel (now dedicated to St. Stephen)

The small church is located on the high moors in a hamlet of three or four houses. It comprises a long narrow nave-cum-sanctuary of five bays. In the keystone above the s. porch are two dates, 1673 and 1834, the latter marking the most recent major restoration when most of the building was reconstructed. There is a w. tower with a saddleback roof. Over the s. doorway inside the nave is a benefaction board dated 1802. The sanctuary possesses a curious-shaped stone altar which is of uncertain age. On the wall nearby is a tablet in memory of a former minister, Revd. Samuel Hall +1779.

Macclesfield, Forest Chapel of St. Stephen.

918737
MACCLESFIELD, St. Michael and All Angels

In the market place in the centre of the town, the church is situated in a lawned churchyard. The building which was originally constructed c.1278 under the patronage of Queen Eleanor consort of Edward I, has been altered and rebuilt several times, much of the medieval fabric having been destroyed in the process. The sw. tower though clad with a C19 exterior, possesses pre-Reformation work which can be attributed to late C13 and C15. The responds of the two arches (late C13) that used to be at the w. end of the nave of the first church are still in position on either side of the tower arch. However, the chief architectural interest is the early C16 Perp. s. porch built by Thomas Savage, archbishop of York. On its w. side it is richly decorated with quatrefoils, mouldings and coats of arms in the Tudor manner. The Savage chapel within the porch is also C16 Perp. The Legh or westerly s. aisle chapel (c.1422) now used as a baptistry, was rebuilt in 1620. The rest of the church dates from 1898-1901 when Sir A. Blomfield engaged in a major restoration. An important single feature of the church are the ancient memorials, the most comprehensive collection in Cheshire. In the C19 chancel, there are two such memorials of which the better includes the effigies of Sir John Savage +1495 and his wife. The two figures lie on an ornate altar-tomb in a tomb recess. The C19 s. aisle is dominated by the imposing monument which stands against the e. wall. This monument by W. Stanton commemorates Thomas Savage, Earl Rivers +1694. The deceased wearing a full-bottomed wig and flowing classical garb, is shown lying on his side propped up by an elbow. His effigy rests on a marble table-tomb and is framed by two pillars and a segmental pediment. The Savage chapel which still retains its medieval altar-slab contains more ancient memorials. These include the famous Pardon Brass in memory of Roger Legh +1506, and the large classical memorial of Sir John Savage +1597. The Legh chapel contains no tombs but several wall tablets of which the most interesting are one to William Legh +1630 with an inscription in three languages, and another to Perkin-a-Legh (undated). The church has a large number of brass chandeliers of which one in the nave is dated 1739 and another, 1822. There is a marble font (1744) with round gadrooned bowl and baluster-stem. Over the w. doorway are the Royal arms (c.1825) and nearby, a C17 churchwardens' pew with a fine oak panelled front. A benefaction board covers the period 1613 to 1863.

Macclesfield St. Michael, Monument of Thomas Savage, Earl Rivers +1694.

486472
MALPAS, St. Oswald

The little town of Malpas is gathered under a small ridge on which is set the church next to the site of the former castle. The church undoubtedly is one of the finest in the county, being built in the w. Cheshire style, mostly in late C15. The handsome pinnacled and embattled exterior is enhanced by two sets of elegant wrought-iron gates (C18) made by the Davies brothers of Bersham. The original C14 plan of the church was adhered to in C15 when the final rebuilding took place involving in particular retention of the tower, the core of the chancel and windows at the ends of the aisles. Since late medieval times the only substantial alteration has been the erection of a vestry (1717) in neo-Classical style by an architect no less than Sir John Vanbrugh. The C14 Dec. w. tower though somewhat plain, has a Dec. great w. window with ten reticulation units renewed by H. Clutton in 1864. The C15 Perp. porch which is well proportioned, consists of two storeys with a C14 Dec. inner doorway. The C15 Perp. nave consists of six bays with n. and s. arcades the piers of which each have eight demi-shafts. Below the n. respond at the e. end, is situated a springer of the former low arcade of C14. The C15 nave roof is a good example of Cheshire work of the period and is of the camber-beam kind enriched with gilded bosses and angels and crows' feet. The font (C15) is octagonal with quatrefoil panels and has an oak cover dated 1627. In the nave floor is a memorial slab of white alabaster bearing the incised effigy of a priest, Urian Davenport +1495. The chancel, remodelled in C15, is divided from the nave by a wide C14 Dec. archway. Above the latter is the large painting by the mid C18 artist Hayman, "St. Peter's Denial". The late C15 Perp. e. window contains stained glass in memory of Bishop Heber whose father was rector. In the chancel is a C14 Dec. triple sedilia and piscina; while against the same wall stand three C15 stalls with misericords. Below the high altar is a treasury or crypt. At the e. end of the C15 Perp. n. aisle is the Cholmondeley chapel. Rare for Cheshire, it contains in its e. wall a Dec. window (c.1300) with geometrical tracery. The chapel is fenced by a late medieval timber screen that bears a Latin inscription stating that the chapel was built in 1514. There is an alabaster tomb-chest in the centre of the chapel on which are the effigies of Sir Hugh Cholmondeley +1596 and his wife. The s. aisle has the Brereton chapel at its e. end which is also fenced by a late medieval timber screen, the latter with an English inscription. The chapel houses an effigied altar-tomb to Sir

Randle Brereton +1530. Also, the chapel has a C14 Dec. triple sedilia and rare double piscina. The s. aisle contains some box-pews (1680) and a superb C13 iron-bound oak chest. The roofs of the two aisles date from C15.

Malpas, St. Oswald.

561457
MARBURY, St. Michael

In a remote corner of s. Cheshire, the church stands proudly by the mere that gives Marbury its name. Most of the building is Perp. and was constructed in the latter half of C15. However, the chancel was rebuilt c.1822 and regothicised by Douglas & Fordham in 1891-92. Before going inside, note that the one clockface that there is on the tower can only be seen from the hall across the mere and not from the village! The ground-floor area of the C15 Perp. tower provides wall-space for a number of benefaction boards with dates ranging from 1601 to 1839. At the e. end of the three-bay C15 Perp. nave is a C15 wooden pulpit carved in typical late Perp. style with panels decorated with crocketed and finialed ogee-tops. The C19 e. window of the chancel is flanked by two early C19 boards on which are inscribed the Ten Commandments etc. Standing at the w. end of the n. aisle is a four-wheeled bier for funerals, made in 1918.

Marbury, Perpendicular pulpit, late C15.

962880
MARPLE, All Saints

The neo-EE. church was built by Medland & Taylor in 1878-80. It retains a C18 font with a gadrooned bowl and baluster stem, a C17 wooden parish chest and a handsome two-tier chandelier (1811). The tower of the former church, built by S. Oldknow in 1808-12, survives as a detached campanile. Its ground-floor houses a number of early C19 wall-memorials. Also here is a tablet dated 1744 marking the curacy of Marple which was financially assisted by money from Queen Anne's Bounty.

850680
MARTON, St. James and St. Paul

One of the best half-timbered churches in Cheshire, the black-and-white building is situated on a small bank at the side of the main road. Said to have been founded in 1343, it is believed to be the oldest timbered church of its kind in Europe, possibly sharing this distinction with Lower Peover. Apart from minor alterations carried out in C19 when new windows were inserted, the only substantial change since C14 has been the rebuilding of the chancel in C18. The most interesting section of the church is the C14 timber tower which is surrounded on three sides by an apron with lean-to roofs. At its foot, there are two badly worn C14 stone effigies of knights thought to represent Sir John Davenport and his son Vivian. Nearby is a benefaction board dated 1705. The C14 three-bay nave has timbered octagonal piers on each side. The ancient roof is supported on king-posts. Above the w. doorway of the nave are the remains of a medieval painting. The C15 font has a plain octagonal shape, set on a new stem and base. The wooden pulpit (1620) has five sides with a double row of panels and some pleasant carving. At the w. ends of the aisles are two large mid C18 boards on which are painted the Ten Commandments and likenesses of Moses and Aaron, the painter being E. Penny of Knutsford. In the s. aisle is an Elizabethan parish chest. The altar cross (C14) was acquired for the church in 1956.

Marton, St. James and St. Paul.

982889
MELLOR, St. Thomas Apostle

The little church stands high on the hillside above the floor of the Goyt valley. Near the tower are two strange memorial stones on which are inscribed enigmatic symbols and words said to be masonic. The short plain w. tower is mainly C16 Perp. The remainder of the church was completely rebuilt in early C19 in a neo-Gothic style. The outstanding feature of the church is the early C14 wooden pulpit, the oldest in England if not in Europe. It is constructed from the trunk of an oak tree and is in the form of six panels, five of which are carved with tracery. The early C12 Norm. font is drum-shaped and decorated with several carved figures. At the e. end of the nave are a few C18 box-pews, and on a wall is the sounding board of a C18 former three-decker pulpit. There is also a benefaction board dated 1760.

704663
MIDDLEWICH, St. Michael and All Angels

A prominent church in the centre of the town near a busy road junction. The building has a long history with fabric surviving from C12, C14, C15/C16 and C19. Of the C12 Norm. church, all that remains are a pair of complete circular piers at the e. end of the nave together with a pair of semi-circular responds, each pier and respond being separated by a small archway. The remaining portions of nave arcades to the w. are C14 Dec. They have octagonal piers, the capitals of which are carved with handsome fleurons. The core of the nw. tower is C14 Dec. with an upper Perp. section built in early C16. The aisles and chancel were rebuilt and the e. chapels constructed in the Perp. style in late C15 or early C16. In 1857-60 J. Clarke renewed all the external stonework and renewed much of the interior. The roof of the chancel though restored in 1951, was erected by Sir William Brereton in 1621. It possesses some well-carved hammerbeams and fine wall-posts, above which are arch-braces and collar-beams. There are a C15/C16 Perp. sedile and piscina, as well as a misericord seat. The altar-rails, like much of the furniture in the church, is Jacobean. The oldest memorial is a brass plaque to Elizabeth Venables +1591. The single most interesting feature of the church are the timber heraldic screens of 1632 and 1633 now attached to the walls of the tower. Unique in Cheshire, these screens were commissioned by Peter Venables and were illuminated by William Smith, Rouge Dragon Pursuivant of Arms. In the late C15 Perp. s. chancel chapel is a C17 wooden chest, and in the s. aisle a rare wooden poor box, dated 1682.

791802
MOBBERLEY, St. Wilfrid

The church is one of several that conform to the type common in e. Cheshire. Thus it has a low clerestory with two-light windows, roofs with deep overhanging eaves and an absence of battlements save on the tower. The building dates mainly from C14 and C15/C16 However, in 1533 the present w. tower was constructed in Perp. style, replacing a ruined detached tower. And at the same time, the nave was extended towards the new tower in order to effect a link-up. In 1889 J.S. Crowther undertook a considerable restoration of the chancel. The e. parts of the nave arcades are C14 Dec. and the w. C16 Perp. On the spandrels of the n. arcade are medieval paintings of which one may be of St. Christopher. The wooden screen (1683) at the front of the bellringers' gallery in the tower comprises a fence of flat balusters. The best feature of the church is the chancel screen, formerly the rood-screen, made in 1500 by Peter Acton. It consists of eight bays separated by delicately moulded shafts. Overhead, the C16 nave roof is developed as a celure above the screen. The fine five-light Dec. e. window of the chancel though heavily restored by Crowther, originally was constructed c.1290 with uncusped intersecting tracery.

995953
MOTTRAM-IN-LONGDENDALE, St. Michael and All Angels

An impressive embattled building standing on a hill, Warhill, above the small town. In the churchyard are two tombstones of note: One records the local bellringer William Harrison +1880; the other is a flat ledger-stone which tells of the body-snatching of Lewis Brierley +1827, aged 15. The church was constructed in the Perp. style in late C15. However in 1854 a major restoration was carried out by E.H. Shellard who reconstructed the nave and erected a clerestory and vestry. The C15 Perp. w. tower is a well-proportioned structure with unusually long belfry windows. The C19 six-bay nave with arcades of five bays to the n. and six to the s., retains its medieval asymmetry. Hanging down is a big two-tier chandelier (1755). Above the chancel arch, there are five C18 painted panels which formerly were a reredos. These include pictures of Moses and Aaron. The C15 Perp. chancel retains its C15 roof which is of arch-brace construction. In the ne. corner of the sanctuary is a slab of stone believed to be the top section of a medieval altar-tomb to a former rector of Mottram, John Picton +1517. It shows the faint outline of a priest wearing eucharistic vestments. Note also in the chancel the ledger-stones, one of which has lettering one foot high! The C15 Perp. Staveley or s. chancel chapel possesses two defaced recumbent stone effigies of Sir Ralph "Old Roe" Staveley (early C15) and his wife. In the C15 s. aisle is a C12 Norm. font in the shape of a large plain stone barrel and not far away a restored wooden coffer (1678). In the C15 Perp. Hollingworth or n. chancel chapel, there is a large piece of monumental masonry displaying the semi-reclining figure of Reginald Bretland +1703. In the n. aisle, also C15 Perp., is a pair of wooden breadshelves dated 1619 and 1737, and a benefaction board covering the period 1693-1737.

653523
NANTWICH, St. Mary the Virgin

The small but historic town is situated four miles from its large neighbour Crewe, jealously guarding its separate identity. The big church, second in importance in the diocese to Chester cathedral and the finest parish church in the county, forms the natural focus of interest in the centre of the town. Most of the building is constructed in the Dec. style, dating from C14. Though the soft sandstone has caused the exterior to wear badly, there survives from this period a profusion of crocketed pinnacles, gabled buttresses and canopied windows especially of the chancel, transepts and tower. However, a small portion of work round the inner part of the w. doorway of the nave may be attributed to C13; while a section of the s. transept as well as the whole of the two-storey porch are C15 Perp. and the clerestory, C16 Perp. In 1855-61, Sir George Gilbert Scott undertook a major restoration when he rebuilt the w. front and renewed many of the parapets. The building is one of only three ancient cruciform churches in Cheshire, the others being the cathedral and Chester St. John Baptist. Its C14 Dec. central tower which is octagonal, is 101 feet high. The C14 Dec. nave has four bays with arches which are embellished with triple-wave mouldings and piers which consist of four round shafts on the cardinal sides separated by four flat projections on the diagonal sides. The nave pulpit (1601) is

Nantwich, early Perpendicular stone pulpit, c.1400.

constructed of timber and was originally part of a three-decker. The nave walls, n. and s., are supported by flying buttresses which run across the C14 Dec. aisles to the outer walls. The C14 Dec. n. transept consists of three bays of which the n. bay used to serve as a chantry chapel. The springers suggest that this chapel may originally have been vaulted. The interstitium under the tower houses a beautiful stone pulpit (c.1400) which is continuous with the surviving lower half of a stone screen leading into the Dec. chancel. The latter dating from the second half of C14 is a sumptuous architectural creation with flowing tracery in its n. and s. windows and a lierne-vaulted stone roof (c.1385). The chancel contains handsome wooden stalls fitted with misericords and spiky canopies (c.1390). The Elizabethan altar-table was given in 1638 by Thomas Clowes. On the s. side of the sanctuary are a superb Dec. sedilia and piscina with nodding-ogee arched canopies, and on the n. side a Dec. Easter sepulchre. In the s. bay of the s. transept is a fine Perp. window divided into eight cusped lights. The roofs of both transepts date from 1577. Of the few tombs in the church, two are in the s. transept, one being of a mutilated effigy to Sir David Craddock +c.1390, and the other a large impressive free-standing monument to Sir Thomas Smith +1614.

Nantwich chancel, stalls and spiky canopies, c.1390.

291774
NESTON, St. Mary and St. Helen

The parish church occupies a prominent site in the middle of this small town on the e. side of the Dee estuary. With the exception of the w. tower, the church was totally rebuilt by J. Francis Doyle in 1874-75. The tower has little architectural refinement, the lowermost section dating from C14 and containing some re-used Norm. masonry. In 1854 it was raised by one stage and this is borne out by the existence of two sets of belfry windows, one above the other. The main part of the building conforms to a neo-EE. design. Arguably the most beautiful artefact of the church is the set of elaborate wrought-iron gates at the entrance to the tower from the nave, commemorating Reginald Bushell +1904. Over the tower archway is a fine carved Royal arms (C17). In the C19 n. chancel chapel, there is an ancient miniature Easter sepulchre set into the n. wall. In the C19 s. aisle are some stone pieces including remains of pre-Norm. carved crosses and a C14 grave-slab with a carved cross fleury commemorating a priest. Nearby is a Jacobean wooden chest and the church's old wrought-iron weathercock which did service from 1747 to 1975. The C16 Perp. font, also in the s. aisle, has an octagonal bowl with quatrefoiled panels.

Nether Alderley interior, Stanley pew, C17.

Nether Alderley exterior, gabled end of Stanley pew (shown to right of picture).

842761
NETHER ALDERLEY, St. Mary

The old schoolhouse (1628) and mausoleum (1909) of the Stanley family provide company for the church which is located at the end of a quiet cul-de-sac. The building which is constructed in the e. Cheshire style, dates mainly from late C15 and early C16, though there are some earlier remnants, especially the s. doorway, which date from C14. The chancel is Victorian, being rebuilt by Cuffley & Starkey in 1856. The upper Stanley pew grafted on to the Perp. s. aisle in C17 is an unusual structure which adds to the picturesque outward (and inward) appearance of the church. The fine C16 Perp. w. tower was probably built by the master-mason who erected the Mobberley tower. The C15/C16 Perp. nave is of four bays with arcades that have octagonal piers and double-chamfered arches. Its barrel-shaped roof is C16 with cambered tie-beams and king-posts. At the w. end of the nave, there is a musicians' gallery (1801) now occupied by the organ. The main items of interest in the C19 chancel are the Victorian tombs of the first two lords Stanley of Alderley who are both displayed in effigy.

In the n. aisle is a C17 altar-table. The church possesses in its s. aisle one of two or three C14 fonts in the county. This one has a plain circular bowl with, originally, four supporting carved heads of which two are missing.

832901
NORTHENDEN, St. Wilfrid

St. Wilfrid's church stands in a squarish churchyard in a small town which is now a suburb of Manchester. The only medieval part of the building is the Perp. w. tower which was constructed c.1500, but which was extensively refaced in C19. The remainder of the church was completely rebuilt by J.S. Crowther in 1876 in a neo-Perp. style. He retained the two late Perp. timber screens which fence the n. and s. chancel chapels. The s. screen which is more elaborate than the n., has Gothic lettering which states that it was erected in 1527 and donated by Robert Honford. It has a top-rail on which is carved a delightful trailing vine. The n. screen is of similar though unstated date and is simpler in design. Both chapels contain numerous wall-tablets to the memory of the Tatton family of Wythenshawe, and the Egertons.

650651
OVER (Winsford), St. Chad

The ancient church was inadvisably lengthened in 1926 when medieval masonry was re-used in the new chancel. Though the lay-out of the building has been altered several times prior to the completion of this latest work, most of the fabric is Perp. belonging to late C15 and the first half of C16. This work includes the nave arcades, the s. aisle, porch and w. tower. Small portions of older (C14) work are visible in the church, for instance the respond in the short length of walling at the w. end of the s. arcade. The C16 Perp. tower which is devoid of pinnacles has a frieze on which are superimposed grotesques. The C16 Perp. porch is two-storeyed, the upper stage projecting over the lower. Inside this lower stage is a large holy water stoup. The C20 chancel is of interest chiefly because of the relocated medieval table-tomb to be found on the n.

side of the sanctuary. It is curious in that it consists of two memorials crudely combined, the stonework to the memory of Hugh Starkey Senr. and the brass plate to the memory of Hugh Starkey Jnr. +1555. The C16 s. aisle possesses some big elliptical Perp. windows in its s. wall. In the w. wall of this aisle is a similar window containing two panels of stained glass taken from the former Christ Church, Winsford. The church also has a heavy timber chest (1750).

Over south aisle, Perpendicular five-light window with elliptical arch, late C15/early C16.

457701
PLEMSTALL, St. Peter

The church is located in a remote rural area not far from Chester. The churchyard is characterised by a number of large table-tombs, especially one of C18 immediately to the e. of the chancel which is devoid of an inscription but which is the last resting place of the Hurlestons of Newton. The building is designed on the two-aisled plan and with the exception of the tower, is Perp. of late C15. The w. tower dates from 1826. Before entering the church, notice the mutilated holy water stoup, s. doorway and door, all of C15. The chief interest inside is the array of carved timberwork which has a linenfold theme. Though the parclose screen dividing the chapel at the e. end of the n. aisle from the chancel as well as fragments of the chancel screen are early C16, nearly all the remaining timberwork which is of a high quality, was carved by Revd. J.H. Toogood, a former rector, over a thirty year period from 1907. The C15 Perp. nave and chancel constitute a through-church of eight

Plemstall, Hurleston tomb to east of chancel, C18.

bays with a roof of the same date which is of hammerbeam and arch-brace construction. Against the w. wall is a panelled churchwardens' pew (1697) and nearby, a large benefaction board giving details of Anne Reece's Charity (1888). The sanctuary rails (early C18) have tall slender balusters. In the C15 Perp. n. aisle stands a three-decker pulpit (1722) which still retains its hour-glass. In the vestry-area of the aisle are two benefaction boards, one dated 1727-39 and the other, 1684. The six-bay roof of the aisle is of the same period as the nave roof and is of a similar type of construction.

945792
POTT SHRIGLEY, St. Christopher

The church is located in a small unspoilt village in the hills of e. Cheshire. The building is small and rather plain with a large w. tower. The fabric is chiefly Perp. of late C15. However, the nave is about one hundred years older (late C14). Indeed, three small diagonal buttresses, two at the w. end and one at the ne. corner of the nave are even older (early C14), indicating that the nave may have started life as a free-standing chapel. It consists of two bays only, the Dec. n. arcade belonging to late C14 and the Perp. s. arcade to late C15. The nave roof, also of C15, is of the camber-beam type with a prominent central gold boss. There is a C18 baluster-type font and some box-pews brought from Gawsworth in C19. Over the chancel arch are the Royal arms of George III (c.1800) carved in wood. The late C15 Perp. chancel has a roof of camber-beam construction which is also original. Of special interest is the lengthy inscription on the s. wall of the chancel to Midshipman Peter Downes +1798. The altar-rails (early C18) have turned balusters. The Perp. n. and s. aisles are of the same date as the chancel.

Pott Shrigley, angle between nave and north side of tower, revealing small buttress of former chapel, C14.

901769
PRESTBURY, St. Peter

The parish church which is located prominently in the centre of the village, is of the e. Cheshire kind. It shares its churchyard with a late C12 Norm. chapel which was its parochial predecessor. The chapel though largely rebuilt, retains its elaborately decorated w. front which includes a unique assembly of seven carved figures in a stone panel over the doorway. The churchyard also contains a handsome sundial (1672) and a C8 Saxon cross which is preserved in a glass case. The C15 Perp. w. tower which has a frieze one quarter of the way up, is well proportioned, and there is a C15 Perp. one-storey porch containing two benefaction boards covering the periods 1629-1777 and 1765-72. Unusually for Cheshire, the church has a C13 EE. nave with five bays. Its arcades are dissimilar with alternate round and octagonal piers and capitals (and a little nailhead moulding) on the n. side; while on the s. side the piers and capitals are more complex. Above is an early C16 Perp. clerestory and a crude tie-beam, strut and collar-beam roof (1674). The spandrels of the arcades are decorated with paintings of the Twelve Apostles (1719). The pulpit (1607) used to be part of a three-decker, and in the centre of the nave is a two-tier

Prestbury, nave clerestory and south aisle, typical of an east Cheshire church.

chandelier (1814). At the entrance to the tower, there is an early C17 Jacobean strapwork screen. Two churchwardens' pews (1707) stand on either side of the tower archway. The chancel though originally C13 EE. has gone through several phases of reconstruction since then. EE. work found mainly on the n. side includes an internal three-light window fronting the organ. The e. window, inserted by Sir G.G. Scott & J.O. Scott, dates from the period 1879-85. There is another two-tier chandelier in the chancel (1712). The C15 Perp. chancel arch is filled with a timber screen (1787) above which are the Royal arms. The s. aisle (C14 Dec.) contains a C13 font, spoilt by being retooled in 1857. The C19 n. aisle possesses four benefaction boards (1701, 1832, 1833 and 1861) and a large wall memorial to Richard Orford +1791. The aisle is divided from the n. chancel chapel by a wooden screen (1744). The church contains a number of incised monumental slabs. In the chancel is the oldest of these, to Reginald Legh +1482, and next to it a stone tablet in memory of Sir Edward Warren of Poynton +1558. Also in the chancel are a shallow canopied arch with a missing altar-tomb said to have been associated with Sir Urian Legh of Adlington +1627, and an alabaster slab to Robert Downes of Shrigley +1495. Near the e. end of the s. aisle is yet another incised alabaster slab recording the memory of Jasper Worth +1572.

375587
PULFORD, St. Mary

The church which stands just inside the border with Wales, is a rebuild by J. Douglas, 1881-84. It has a sundial, dated 1702, which is set on a square column of stone moulded on each side.

809847
RINGWAY, St. Mary

A redundant church now used as a furniture repository. Close to Manchester airport by the "Romper" Inn, it was built by Preston & Vaughan in 1894-95. Its one distinguishing feature is a picturesque w. end which has a half-timbered gable. The well-maintained churchyard still accommodates many gravestones.

742837
ROSTHERNE, St. Mary

The church is situated in a magnificent elevated position above a large mere. Though much restored, its timber lichgate (1640) is probably the most ancient in the county. The oldest part of the building is on the n. side and it includes the n. arcade (C13 EE.), portions of the C14 Dec. n. aisle and the n. chancel chapel. The remainder is C16 Perp., except for the w. tower (1742-44) and the chancel and vestry (both by Sir A.W. Blomfield in 1888). The s. arcade of the nave (late C15 Perp.) is considerably taller than the n. arcade. In the nave are five churchwardens' staves dated 1833 and marked with William IV's monogram. The chancel contains the C13 recumbent effigy of a knight in semi-relief, possibly Sir Hugh Venables. In the n. chancel chapel are several C18 and early C19 wall memorials to members of the Brooke and other families. In the C16 Perp. s. chancel chapel is a most impressive and substantial monument which stands against the e. wall. Erected by J. Bacon in 1792 and constructed of white marble, it commemorates S. Egerton +1780. In the same area of the church is a free-standing table-tomb on which rests the effigy of Charlotte Egerton +1845, by R. Westmacott, Jnr.

511833
RUNCORN, All Saints

Located close to the bridge over the River Mersey opposite Widnes, the church is designed in a neo-EE. style by A. Salvin and dates from 1847-49. It contains a number of artefacts which predate the Victorian building. Chief of these are a C12 Norm. grave slab, a late C17 holy table, a C18 wooden chest with drawers below, the Royal arms of George III (early C19) and an undated benefaction board (c.1700). The main interest of the building comprise the numerous and varied C18 and C19 wall memorials, many of which record the passing of members of the Brooke family.

984766
SALTERSFORD,
Jenkin Chapel of St. John Baptist

The little church stands in isolation on the moors of e. Cheshire. If it were not for its saddleback roofed tower (1754-55), the main part of the building (1733) would look like a house. It has small square windows in two tiers, and a gabled roof of Kerridge slabs. The interior possesses a w. gallery on the front of which are displayed the Stopford arms. The fittings and furniture all belong to C18 — a two-decker pulpit, turned baluster rails at the entrance to the sanctuary, box-pews and a stone font with oak cover.

759608
SANDBACH, St. Mary

When drastically restored by Sir G.G. Scott in 1847-49, the church received a new tower said to be an exact copy of the Perp. former one. The building stands in the middle of the small town, just off the market square where are the famous Saxon crosses. The nave has C15 Perp. arcades and a clerestory modernised in C19. The roof dated 1661 is substantially original with camber-beams and panelling. At the w. end are two fonts: One of Caen stone is by Thomas Stringer (1859), the other (C17) octagonal and decorated with acanthus leaves. In the C19 chancel are six C13 sculptured corbel-heads. The late C15 n. aisle is rich in wall memorials, particularly a three-quarter length marble carving by G.F. Watts, R.A., to Revd. John Armitstead, vicar, +1865. The n. aisle roof (C17) incorporates a carving of the Leversage arms in a wreath. The s. aisle is C15 Perp., but the two-storey s. porch was totally rebuilt in C19.

432502
SHOCKLACH, St. Edith of Polesworth

A little church standing on its own among trees in the fields near the River Dee. It consists of a mid C12 Norm. nave and an early C14 Dec. chancel. The Norm. s. doorway of the nave has a semi-circular arch with a thick hoodmould on which is a chevron-moulding. The C15 font is heptagonal. Over the w. end of the nave are the Royal arms of George III (1760), and a hatchment of the Puleston family. The pulpit (1687) has five plain panels. The C14 Dec. chancel arch is almost semi-circular. The e. window is also C14 Dec. with three cusped lights. The C18 altar-rails possess balusters.

337718
SHOTWICK, St. Michael

Shotwick, St. Michael.

A small church in a dormant village down on the marshlands of the upper Dee estuary. The C12 nave and part of the chancel are Norm., but they were remodelled during C14 when extensions on the n. side of the church were carried out. The Perp. w. tower is late C15. An important feature of the building is the C12 Norm. s. doorway which possesses a semi-circular arch of three orders. On the inside wall of the tower are the Royal arms (1726) of George I. The nave and chancel constitute a through-church. The arcade separating the nave from the n. aisle is C14 Dec. The nave contains some box-pews (c.1706) and a C14 octagonal font. In the chancel is a C14 Dec. e. window of three lights and a C12 Norm. priest's s. doorway. The altar-rails (late C17, even c.1700) have well-turned balusters, and there is also in the chancel a rare C18 single-tier chandelier. The C14 n. aisle possesses a three-decker pulpit (1812); while at the w. end is an impressive churchwardens' pew dated 1673 and four blackened wall boards (1752) displaying the Ten Commandments etc. In the e. window of the C14 Dec. n. chancel chapel, there are some pieces of C14 stained glass which have the "Annunciation" as their subject.

846708
SIDDINGTON, All Saints

A timber-framed church consisting of chancel, nave and bell-turret above the w. end. The chancel which has a quaint overhanging e. gable, can be safely dated as c.1513. The core of the nave, also timber-framed, is of the same age, but it was encased in red brick c.1815. Internally, the nave walls are painted in a black-and-white patterning which gives an unattractive appearance to this section of the building. The w. gallery dates from 1786 and the octagonal font was installed in 1792. The arch-brace roof of the nave contains much original timber (C16). The wooden pulpit (1633) is entered through an opening in the chancel screen. The latter (C16) started life as a rood-screen. In the e. wall of the chancel are some tracery panels which may have originally formed part of the rood-loft parapet. The chancel has a roof most of which is C16 in date.

Siddington, All Saints.

815648
SOMERFORD, Chapel of All Saints

A chapel of ease since 1943, it was built in 1725 by Peter Shakerley as a domestic chapel. It stands in the fields of the former Somerford Hall estate. In the churchyard immediately to the e. of the building is a plain memorial slab surrounded by railings above the grave of the same Peter Shakerley +1726. The chapel is built of chequer brick and is five bays long with semi-circular windows occupying the n. and s. wall-space, bays 1 to 4. The chapel is entered via the w. doorway over which is an inscription and the date of construction. At the w. end is a gallery, and the walls are lavishly panelled internally giving the whole a dignified appearance. The most striking feature of the chapel is the stained glass of the altered e. window (1919), inserted as a memorial to three members of the Shakerley family who died in the Great War, 1914-18. On the n. side of the altar is a fine C17 wall memorial with twisted columns to Elizabeth Shakerley +1691. The panelled timber pulpit, said to have been originally part of a three-decker, is coeval with the building.

423733
STOAK, St. Lawrence

The cruciform church which has a tower at the w. end, is located on the edge of the small village. The building was largely reconstructed by G. Edgecumbe in 1827, the tower and s. transept being totally rebuilt, the C15 nave partly rebuilt and a n. transept erected for the first time. The tower possesses a one-handed clock and in its great w. window is some stained glass featuring the Royal arms of Queen Victoria (1844). The parapet of the w. gallery incorporates panels of the early C16 rood-screen dado; while in the gallery is an early C19 wooden board giving details of the 1827 restoration. There is a large oaken chest with four locks dated 1686. In the C15 Perp. chancel are altar-rails with heavy twisted balusters (early C17). On the n. wall, there is a marble cartouche (1668), the best of its kind in Cheshire, commemorating Henry Bunbury Esq., +1664. The church possesses the largest collection of Randle Holme wooden heraldic memorial tablets, eleven in all, most of which record the demise of members of the Bunbury family.

898905
STOCKPORT, St. Mary

Standing on a prominent hillock in the middle of the town, the church was largely rebuilt in 1813-17 to a neo-Gothic design by Lewis Wyatt. However, the chancel and small n. chancel chapel are original (C14 Dec.). At the e. end of the chancel (c.1310) is a Dec. window of six cusped lights with flowing tracery. On the s. side of the sanctuary is a handsome Dec. triple sedilia and nearby a Dec. double piscina. Against the n. wall of the sanctuary, there is an Easter sepulchre which houses the badly preserved monument to Richard de Vernon, rector, 1306-34. He is shown in effigy. Also in the chancel is a brass wall tablet to John Wainwright +1768, the composer of the hymn-tune "Christians awake, salute the happy morn". There is a rare C14 single-framed timber roof above the chancel. Attached to one of the nave piers is the remnant of an Elizabethan panelled and fluted pulpit (dated 1598); while over the chancel arch are the Royal arms of George III.

Stockport St. Mary, Decorated chancel, c.1310.

894904
STOCKPORT, St. Peter

A large brick church built in 1768 by William Wright. The chancel dating from 1888, is surprisingly in keeping with the remainder of the building. The turret clock (1769) is claimed to be the oldest public clock in Greater Manchester. There is a large wall memorial with garlanded urn to William Wright +1770. Also, there is a C18 (or early C19) hatchment to a member of the same family.

801672
SWETTENHAM, St. Peter

The church is located in a remote village at the centre of a maze of minor roads in e. Cheshire. The building was originally constructed of timber and plaster c.1300, and of this there remain the brick-encased n. aisle and chancel walls together with some of the timberwork of the roofs of the chancel and nave. The brick w. tower dates from 1721-22 when the task of encasing was carried out. The nave arcades were constructed in a neo-Norm. style by J.M. Derrick in 1846. The s. aisle was rebuilt in stone c.1865. The roof of the nave, drastically restored in C19, is of the tie-beam and king-post type. At the w. end of the nave is a C18 font and at the e. end an early C18 panelled pulpit. In the chancel, there are some C18 altar-rails placed round the three sides of the sanctuary.

553625
TARPORLEY, St. Helen

Located halfway along the village street, the church displays many outward signs of having been extensively restored in C19. Indeed this work was undertaken by J.S. Crowther in 1861-78 when all the fabric was rebuilt save the C14 Dec. nave arcades and the late C15 Perp. n. and s. chancel chapels. These arcades are somewhat unusual in that whereas the n. possesses the usual octagonal piers, the s. arcade has rare hexagonal ones. The nave is divided from the chancel by a fine wrought-iron screen (1891) within which are set some C16 gates brought from a church in Italy. In the Utkington or n. chancel chapel is a full length effigy in marble of Sir John Crewe +1711; while an adjacent monument consists of an altar-tomb to Mary Crewe +1690 and two female relatives. The baptistry (1931) contains a plain C15 octagonal font.

Tarporley, south chancel chapel, Perpendicular window with segmental arch, late C15.

492670
TARVIN, St. Andrew

Hemmed in by houses, the church is dominated by a handsome late C15/early C16 Perp. w. tower. Built of red standstone, this tower displays some elaborate decorative work on its w. side including a quatrefoiled frieze, a canopied doorway and some niches. The oldest parts of the church are the C14 Dec. s. aisle, s. arcade and tower arch. The n. aisle which possesses some elegant Perp. windows, and the n. arcade were constructed at the same time as the tower. The chancel though rebuilt in C18, was finally remodelled by G.E. Grayson & E.A. Ould in 1891-92. The nave which has a C15/C16 Perp. n. arcade and a C14 Dec. arcade on the

s. side, possesses two C18 collecting shovels; while hanging between the nave and chancel is a C18 two-tier chandelier. The roof of the nave which dates from 1650, is of hammerbeam and arch-brace type with moulded wall-brackets and pendants. The eight-panelled reredos (c.1500) is thought to be Flemish in origin. The oldest monument in the church is a brass tablet on the n. wall of the chancel which commemorates a former mayor of Chester, Henry Hardware +1584. The s. aisle which includes the Bruen chapel at its e. end, possesses a rare C14 single-framed roof. One of the most valuable possessions of the church is a C14 wooden screen that divides the chapel from the remainder of s. aisle. Near the screen high on the wall is the medieval carved stone figure known as the "Tarvin Imp". There are three Randle Holme wooden heraldic tablets on the wall of the s. chapel.

Tarvin tower, Perpendicular west doorway, late C15/early C16.

486586
TATTENHALL, St. Alban

The well cared for churchyard is entered through some handsome wrought-iron gates; it contains a fine sundial (1822). Though the early C16 Perp. w. tower is original, most of the remainder of the church was rebuilt by J. Douglas in 1869-70. Thus the whole of the chancel and nave belong to this latter period. However, large portions of the n. and s. aisles are part of the C16 Perp. edifice. In the ringers' gallery are two benefaction boards dated 1712 and 1802. The roof of the nave consists of a C19 scissor-brace and arch-brace construction. Hanging in the centre of the nave is a beautiful two-tier chandelier (1755). In a s. window of the chancel are some pieces of medieval glass (C14?) portraying the figures of St. Alban and St. Stephen and displaying the monogram of St. Mary the Virgin.

Tattenhall churchyard, neo-Classical sundial, 1822.

007798
TAXAL, St. James

The hamlet and little church are located on a hillside among tall trees. To the e. of the chancel is a curious canopied table-tomb erected in memory of Elizabeth Shallcross +C17. The plain w. tower dates chiefly from early C16. The nave was rebuilt in 1825 and the chancel in 1889. On the n. wall of the nave is a tablet commemorating Michael Heathcote +1768, "Gentleman of the Pantry and Yeoman of the Mouth to his late Majesty King George the second". Over the s. doorway are the Royal arms of Queen Anne (c.1710). On either side of the tower arch are C18 boards displaying the Ten Commandments, etc. In the ground-floor area of the tower, there are benefaction boards bearing dates 1776, 1793 and 1886; while lower down are several C17 and C18 ledger-stones with large letter inscriptions. The oak panelling of the sanctuary bears the date 1694.

650875
THELWALL, All Saints

A medium sized church in an undistinguished village where it is surrounded by modern housing not far from the famous M6 viaduct. The nave of J. Mountford Allen dates from 1843, though it was lengthened at both ends later. The chancel is of 1857; while the n. aisle and possibly the w. porch were constructed in 1890 by W. Owen.

442746
THORNTON-LE-MOORS, St. Mary

Its environs enroached on by an oil refinery, the old church is situated in a somewhat gaunt burial ground devoid of trees. The sandstone building which is of the two-aisled type, consists of C14 Dec. nave, chancel and s. aisle; while the s. chancel chapel and sw. tower are early C16 Perp. The s. porch (c.1700) possesses a surprisingly large C14 Dec. inner doorway with continuous small and large recessed quadrant mouldings, and a door dated 1725. The C14 Dec. arcade dividing the nave from the s. aisle, has octagonal piers and arches with double-chamfered mouldings. There are two fonts, one dated 1673 and another of C18 vintage. The chancel is almost as big as the nave. In its e. wall is a large C14 Dec. window of five cusped lights and with some curious flowing tracery. The C16 hammerbeam roof of the chancel is the only surviving medieval one in the church. The chancel possesses a holy table and twisted baluster rails, both of 1694. Unusually, the rails enclose the sanctuary on three sides. There are six C17 Randle Holme heraldic wooden tablets in the nave and chancel, mostly to the memory of members of the Bunbury family. Other memorials include some C19 brightly coloured hatchments of the Perryns. At the e. end of the s. aisle, there is a C14 piscina. The tower archway is filled with a timber screen comprising both a benefaction board (1898) and a board giving details of Anne Hodgkinson's Charity (1887).

439456
THREAPWOOD, St. John

A small church in a remote corner of sw. Cheshire. The pure Georgian building of 1815 looks like a house, being rectangular in shape and constructed of brick with two rows of square-topped windows. Galleries run round three sides of the five-bay interior. The church contains two brass single-tier chandeliers (1817). The altar is backed by four panels on which are written the Ten Commandments, etc. Also, the altar is fenced by a three-sided set of iron altar-rails. Both these and the panels are coeval with the building.

247841
THURSTASTON, St. Bartholomew

The prominently sited church was designed and constructed by J.L. Pearson, the architect of Truro cathedral, in 1885. It conforms to a neo-EE. style. The tower of the former small church (1824) shares the later church's burial ground. In the latter, there remain several C17 gravestones including a flat memorial to Revd. Robert Bradshaw +1689. Also, outside the church is a C17 Restoration stone font with an octagonal bowl and round stem, and the ancient stone coffin-lid of a child. In the church are the Royal arms of Queen Anne (c.1707), a breadshelf (1723) and a C17 parish chest. Wall memorials include several of C18 and C19.

457506
TILSTON, St. Mary

A remote village near the River Dee, its church located on the sw. outskirts. Instead of a lichgate, there is a handsome gateway (1687) with heavy wrought-iron gates (1826). The church was heavily restored in 1879. However, earlier surviving fabric includes the late C15 Perp. w. tower, considerable portions of the C16 Perp. nave, and the C17 n. nave chapel. The four-bay nave is entered through a C16 n. doorway which has a Tudor head and a square label. Above the inside of this doorway is a carved beam (dated 1618) bearing the name of Sir Peter Warburton and his wife Alice. Nearby is a C13 coffin-lid with a floriated cross. The octagonal pulpit is early Georgian. There is a benefaction board (1841) on the wall of the ground-floor area of the tower. The C19 chancel has a fine Elizabethan carved and painted roof, communion rails (1677) with flat openwork balusters, and a holy table (also 1677).

527463
TUSHINGHAM, Old Church of St. Chad

The nave and chapel of this little picturesque church are built as one in brick, 1689-91, through money donated by John Dod, a London mercer. The furnishings and fittings (C17) are all original and intact i.e. bench-pews, flat-baluster chancel screen, two high-backed family pews, a plain panelled pulpit, and a holy table with front turned legs and carved top-rails. Besides these, there are a handsome benefaction board with painted putto (1689), a C17 Jacobean font of wood, and an achievement of the Vernon family painted on a small board. There are several early C19 wall memorials. The hearse-house (1834) contains the parish hearse.

Tushingham Old Church, hearse-house, 1834.

772736
UPPER PEOVER, St. Lawrence

Situated in parkland close to Peover hall, the church is surrounded by a variety of trees. An attractive sundial stands by the short path leading to the churchyard. The church is mostly — though not entirely — constructed of brick, the w. tower dating from 1739-41, and the nave and chancel by William Turner from 1811. However, smaller sections of the church are older. Thus the n. chancel chapel (the Mainwaring mortuary chapel) was built in 1648 in a pure classical style, and the Perp. s. porch and Perp. s. nave chapel were constructed in mid C15. On the w. wall of the nave is a board displaying a fine version of the Royal arms of Charles II (1661) and near the s. door the remnants of a C15 holy water stoup. On the n. wall hang the "Stars and Stripes" presented in 1944 by Gen. George Patton. The nave also contains two churchwardens' staves (c.1833) marked with William IV's monogram, a handsome C17 wooden pulpit and a C15 Perp. font.

The recessed effigied tomb of Sir Randle Mainwaring +c.1456 is located in the s. nave chapel. Like other effigies of the Mainwaring family in this church and elsewhere, Sir Randle's lies with a donkey's head as a headrest. The chapel has a C20 wooden reredos consisting of three panels painted by Miss M. Elsdale after the style of Italian masters. In the C19 chancel is a table-tomb on which rest alabaster effigies probably of Sir John Mainwaring +c.1483 and his wife. The C20 timber screen dividing the chancel from the n. chancel chapel was designed by F.H. Crossley. The chief memorial in this chapel is a tomb-chest carved with heraldic symbols on which rest the effigies of Philip Mainwaring +1647 and his wife. Also in the chapel are two finely incised C16 alabaster slabs to other members of the family; while on the e. wall is another tablet, this in memory of Sir John Mainwaring +1702.

Upper Peover, sundial at entrance to churchyard, 1717.

296922
WALLASEY, St. Hilary

The churchyard stands on a windswept hillside which is treeless. Apart from the tower, the old church was destroyed by fire in 1857. A new cruciform building was erected some fifty yards to the n. in 1858-59 by W. & J. Hay in a neo-Gothic style. The now-detached medieval tower consists of three stages of which the lowest is C14 Dec. and the upper two early C16 Perp.

697896
WARBURTON, Old Church of St. Werburgh

The ancient building now redundant is situated near the River Mersey, standing in a tree-filled churchyard in which is a handsome sundial (1765). The plan of the church is somewhat strange, there being a tower at the e. end. The oldest part of the building is the nave together with its attendant aisles, of which the half-timbered n. wall and wooden nave piers may well be medieval. The remainder of the nave which is constructed of ashlar, dates from 1645, and the n. chancel aisle, also of ashlar, was constructed later in the same century. In 1711 the chancel, se. tower, and s. chancel transept were built of brick. The church retains a large octagonal stone font which is inscribed "William Drinkwater the Keeper 1603". The chancel is surrounded on three sides by a C17 wooden half-screen, as well as a wooden holy table and pulpit of similar date. In the floor of the chancel are several ledger-stones marking the resting places of former incumbents. On the floor of the s. aisle is a big C12/C13 stone coffin.

709610
WARMINGHAM, St. Leonard

The church is located in a small village near Crewe. Its w. tower built in 1715, was regothicised in 1899. The remainder of the church was rebuilt in neo-Perp. style by R.C. Hussey in 1870. The churchyard retains its C18 round sundial stem. Inside the church is a wooden benefaction board (1755) and several old wall memorials. The latter include a handsome cartouche to William Vernon +1732, a rectangular brass plate to Revd. William Lingards +1620, a marble tablet with oval panel to Revd. Randulph Crewe +1777, and another marble tablet to Ralph Vernon +1798.

462633
WAVERTON, St. Peter

The main part of the church dates mainly from C16. However, much of the n. side was reconstructed in 1888. The C16 Perp. w. tower which is disproportionately large compared with the remainder of the building, is topped with a C19 cap and embattled parapet. An outstanding feature of the tower is its Perp. w. doorway with Tudor arch set in a square frame. The ground-floor area of the tower serves as a porch, on the walls of which are the Royal arms of Charles II (1663) and a benefaction board (1704). The three-bay nave though largely C19 now retains its original C14 Dec. piers and capitals. Its roof which is arch-braced and with collar-beams, is dated 1635. There is a handsome memorial tablet in the C16 Perp. s. aisle to William Dutton +1762. He was faithful steward to the Massie family for fifty years, and in recognition of this, he and his descendants were given the right of burial in the Massie family vault. An unusual feature of the building is the timber-framing of the chancel which probably dates from C16 or C17.

617743
WEAVERHAM, St. Mary the Virgin

A fine building in an otherwise unremarkable large village. It is one of the few medieval churches in Cheshire that was built almost in its entirety as a Perp. edifice during late C15 and early C16. The late C15 Perp. w. tower is well proportioned and has a frieze below the parapet. The C16 Perp. nave and chancel comprise a through-church of five bays, the arcades of which have wide Tudor arches. The plain octagonal font which has an original cover probably dates from mid C17. The C16 Perp. e. window of the chancel contains five uncusped main lights with subarcuated tracery in its head. Below are two rows of C16 wooden panelling carved with a linenfold motif. There is a handsome altar-table (c.1736) with claw-feet and cabriole legs, and some wooden altar-rails (1708) with twisted balusters. On either side of the chancel are parclose screens dated 1636. In the C16 Perp. s. chancel chapel and s. aisle which are partially occupied by C18 box-pews, are several memorials to the local branch of the Wilbraham family. At the w. end is a wooden pew incorporating material from the medieval former rood-screen. The roof of the n. side of the church which is of the camber-beam type, is the only original one and dates from C16.

218864
WEST KIRBY, St. Bridget

The parish church is situated in a well-wooded area of the town. Although possessing a long history, the building was drastically restored in 1869-70 by Messrs. Kelly & Edwards of Chester who completely rebuilt the nave, built a new s. aisle and s. porch, and partially rebuilt the chancel. The old parts of the church are the C15 Perp. tower, C16 Perp. n. aisle, and sections of the C14 Dec. chancel and n. chancel chapel. The w. tower has a handsome embellished w. doorway which is placed under a label terminating in plain stops. There is a gilded weathervane possessing the date 1757. The three-bay chancel retains much of its C14 Dec. work on the s. and e. sides. Curiously, there is a C14 priest's doorway on the s. side which has a normal door on the outside but is blocked with stone on the inside. The arresting painting (1906) over the chancel arch and wrought-iron screen are by C.E. Kempe who is said to have been responsible for the stained glass in nineteen out of the twenty three windows in the building. Possibly the finest of these is his "Tree of the Church" glass (1883) in the e. window of the chancel. On the s. wall of the chancel is a sandstone tablet to the memory of Johannes Vanzoelen +1689. On the n. wall of the C14 Dec. n. chancel chapel are two C18 memorials to members of the Glegg family. The early C16 e. window of this chapel is a noteworthy feature of the church. The C19 s. porch has head-stops thought to be likenesses of Queen Victoria and William Jacobson who was bishop of Chester.

628694
WHITEGATE, St. Mary

In an idyllic setting, the small church stands opposite the historic gateway leading to the former abbey of Vale Royal. On the s. side of the churchyard are some ornate wrought-iron gates hung between stone pillars (1736). Of the original medieval church only the C15 timber piers of the nave survive. The s. doorway dates from 1728, and the remainder was rebuilt in 1874-75 by J. Douglas. Over the C19 tower arch are the Royal arms of Charles II (1660). In the C19 chancel is an ambitious stone reredos installed in 1876-77 in memory of a former vicar. The C19 n. chancel chapel contains wall tablets in memory of the barons Delamere. There is some notable stained glass by E. Frampton in one of the windows of the C19 n. aisle. Installed to mark the sixtieth year of the reign of Queen Victoria in 1897, it depicts "Christ in Judgment". In the C19 nw. vestry is a benefaction board (1710).

848815
WILMSLOW, St. Bartholomew

On a bank above the River Bollin, the church displays little external embellishment save on the w. tower and s. porch both restored in Victorian days. The building is a mixture of styles and dates as the following summary shows: The w. tower is C15 Perp. with a C19 parapet and w. doorway; the nave arcades are late C14 Dec. with an early C16 Perp. clerestory; the n. and s. aisles are a mixture of late C14 Dec., and C15 and C16 Perp.; the n. and s. chancel chapels are early C16 Perp; the chancel is a mixture of early C16 Perp. and C19; the s. aisle chapel is c.1700; and the s. porch which may have been originally C16 Perp. is now C19. The oldest part of the church is the EE. e. crypt (c.1220) entered by a door to the s. of the high altar. The Dec. piers of two similar arcades of the five-bay nave are octagonal with simple capitals and double-chamfered pointed arches. The nave roof though extensively restored in C19 can still be classed as medieval as it retains much of its original timberwork. It is of the camber-beam kind with eighteen panels to each of its five bays. In the ground-floor area of the tower are two benefaction boards, one dated 1825 and the other undated (c.1800). The C19 chancel screen contains some older timber material. However the parclose screens nearby are ancient (C16 Perp.). The arcades of the chancel consist of wide four-centred arches (c.1522). On the n. side of the sanctuary is the tomb of Henry Trafford +1537, former rector and benefactor of the church. He is depicted wearing ecclesiastical robes and with his head resting on a book. At the e. end of the chancel is a Perp. five-light window. The Trafford or n. chancel chapel contains two ogee-arched recesses in its n. wall housing the tombs and effigies of Humphrey Newton +1536 and his wife. At the w. end of the chapel is a large parish chest (1633). An early C16 wooden screen with a trailing vine divides the chapel from the adjacent n. aisle. The chief item of interest in the Booth or s. chancel chapel is the monumental brass to Sir Robert Del Booth +1460. Of good quality, it is the oldest brass in the county and shows the knight wearing C15 plate armour and his lady a long flowing gown. The chapel is separated from the s. aisle by another C16 wooden screen. The s. aisle chapel retains its original (c.1700) furniture of wall-panelling and box-pews.

Wilmslow, north chancel chapel, Perpendicular window with square head and five cuspless lights, early C16.

959661
WINCLE, St. Michael

A small church located in the Peak area of se. Cheshire. A date of 1647 over the s. doorway of the chancel, and a doorway of similar age leading into the s. side of the nave provide evidence as to the oldest portions of the building. However, the nave and chancel were heavily restored and their windows regothicised by E. Witts in 1882. The embattled w. tower dates from c.1820. Inside the nave, there is a painting showing what the church looked like before the Victorian restoration.

682536
WISTASTON, St. Mary the Virgin

The present church is by G. Latham of Nantwich and was constructed in 1827-28. The chancel was lengthened and the s. transept added in 1884. There is a big baluster-stem of a sundial (1817). Little of antiquarian interest survives within the church save a three-lock wooden parish chest (1684) and several C19 wall memorials.

665739
WITTON (Northwich), St. Helen

Standing on a prominent site in the centre of the town by a busy relief road, the church is constructed in the w. Cheshire style with large Perp. windows and a profusion of battlements on the parapets of the nave, aisles, chapels and porch. The present building dates from C14 though little of the Dec. fabric of that period remains. Indeed since then there have been a number of substantial alterations to the design affecting in particular the chancel and the location of the n. arcade of the nave. The greater part of the church — that is, the tower, w. section of the chancel, nave clerestory, s. aisle, s. chancel chapel and s. porch — is Perp., dating from late C15 and early C16. During subsequent centuries, especially C19, the apse was rebuilt (1861) and the n. aisle widened (1884) (the latter being effected by Paley & Austin). The fine Perp. w. tower (c.1498) was erected by Thomas Hunter, the builder of the tower at Great Budworth. He retained the tower arch and its surround which dates from C14. The five-bay nave consists of two C14 Dec. arcades of which the n. arcade was moved four feet to the n. during the later Perp. reconstruction when the clerestory was built. The most splendid feature of the church is the nave roof of c.1525. Of the camber-beam type, it possesses gorgeous large and small gilded bosses with elaborate carvings on the principal beams. The Royal arms (c.1801) are displayed on a wall in the ground-floor area of the tower. At the entrance to the chancel is a C16 vice on the n. side which used to afford access to the rood-loft; and opposite it on the s. side is a C14 respond of a former chancel arch. The s. chancel chapel (now the lady chapel) possesses a C15 e. window of five cusped lights, a window which appears to have been reversed. Below it is a rare C14 Dec. stone reredos which has a row of twelve ogee-headed niches formerly containing statuettes.

Witton, St. Helen.

275869
WOODCHURCH, Holy Cross

Overlooking the motorway, the church is located in a leafy oasis among housing estates. The oldest part is the C12 Norm. chancel which is considerably out of line with the nave. In the n. wall is a transitional Norm. window (C12) which is splayed and of a single light. Over it and built into the wall is a C13 wheel-cross. The chancel arch and e. window are C14 Dec. In the latter are eight stained glass medallions of Flemish origin (c.1650) surrounding a central panel depicting the "Crucifixion" scene. On the n. side of the chancel are three C17 Randle Holme wooden heraldic tablets. Two desks with panelled oak fronts possess four bench-ends (c.1400) with poppyheads. Probably the outstanding feature of the church is the modern rood-screen. Carved in Barnston oak by A. Durst to a design by B.A. Millar, it commemorates Blanche Burroughs +1929. The C14 Dec. w. tower has two massive diagonal buttresses on its w. side. The handsome s. porch is Perp., dating from C16. The s. wall of the nave above the arcade on that side dates from C12. However, the four-bay arcade below is C14 Dec. At its e. end is a small medieval doorway which gave access to the altar of the s. chapel. The n. arcade was constructed in 1964-65 when the n. aisle was built. Near the organ screen at the w. end of the nave is an ancient parish chest with three locks and a benefaction board (1741). Though the s. aisle belongs to C14, its Perp. windows were inserted in C16. Two wooden breadshelves carry the dates 1641 and 1670. The C20 n. aisle possesses much re-used Norm. masonry and some C17 windows. The C15 font has an octagonal bowl with angel-corbels underneath.

079995
WOODHEAD, St James

The existing small isolated building dates from C18.

594478
WRENBURY, St. Margaret

In the centre of the village is the green, and at the side of this is the church and churchyard. Apart from the chancel rebuilt in 1806 (and regothicised in 1865) and the s. porch rebuilt in 1795, the church is of one period and design: i.e. early C16 Perp. The nave of five bays has a C18 gallery at its w. end on which gallery is mounted the organ. The nave roof (C16) is constructed of tie-beams and collar-beams. On the walls above the arcades are two C18 hatchments of the Cotton family. The handsome box-pews (c.1700) which fill the body of the church, have crests on their doors. The pulpit is Georgian, and near it is a long timber chest bound with iron strips. In the s. aisle is a curious dog-whippers pew (c.1734). The main area of interest is undoubtedly the chancel which contains a large collection of memorials, mostly to Cottons and Starkeys of C18 and C19. Chief of these is an inscribed table-tomb to Stapleton Cotton, Viscount Combermere +1865.

700499
WYBUNBURY, St. Chad.

Built in the mid seventies on a virgin site, the modernistic church is located along the main street of the village some two or three hundred yards from the old churchyard. The late C15 Perp. tower is the sole surviving part of the former church. Ninety six feet high, it has an elegant appearance with crocketed pinnacles, gargoyles, a frieze and an impressively decorated w. doorway.

11. GLOSSARY OF TERMS

ABACUS (pl. Abaci)
A flat stone forming the topmost member of a capital or decorated head placed above a pier, column, shaft or pilaster.

ACANTHUS LEAF
A thick leaf used for decoration on Norman capitals.

ACHIEVEMENT OF ARMS
A complete display of armorial bearings often appearing on monuments.

ANNULET
A small ring of stone encircling a column, usually to mask a join.

ARCH-BRACE
A curved piece of timber used to stiffen or bind roof-members.

ARCH-SHAPES
(See Appendix).

ASHLAR
Blocks of stone, cut to even faces and right-angled edges, put together in horizontal courses and used inside or outside.

BALLFLOWER
An ornament resembling a three-petalled flower having the shape of a ball.

BASE-MOULD
A horizontal line of projecting stonework which may be highly moulded, located near ground-level external to the building.

BILLET
A pattern of moulding developed and commonly used in the Norman period. It consists of a series of short raised rectangles or squares which may be repeated in several bands.

BOSS
An embellished block of timber or stone at the intersection of the ribs of a vault.

CABLE
A pattern of moulding resembling twisted rope, often used on Norman arches, etc.

CAMBER-BEAM
A horizontal length of timber spanning the space between the tops of two parallel walls which is slightly arched to prevent sagging.

CARDINAL SIDES
The north, south, east and west sides of piers, as opposed to the diagonal sides (i.e. north east, south east, north west and south west).

CARTOUCHE
A wall tablet with an ornate scrolled frame.

CASEMENT
A deep wide concave moulding, often enriched, found on the jambs of doors and windows, and on piers. It was commonly employed in Perpendicular architecture.

CAVETTO
A hollow moulding in the form of a quadrant or quarter-circle.

CELURE
The richly panelled, moulded and/or painted roof above an altar or rood.

CHAMFER
A flat surface which is bevelled or pared off an arris (the latter being the sharp edge at the junction of two surfaces). A hollow chamfer has a concave surface.

CHEVRON
A moulding of zig-zag pattern found on Norman arches, etc.

CLASPED BUTTRESS
A buttress which encases the angle or corner of a building on its two sides.

CLERESTORY
The upper storey of the walls of part of a church containing rows of windows expressely inserted to give additional illumination.

CORBEL-TABLE
A series of stone brackets (or corbels) located in close proximity with one another immediately below the roof-line within or without the building and designed to support a parapet. Characteristic of the Norman period.

CROCKET
A decorative feature carved of stone or wood consisting of a projecting bud. Crockets are frequently placed at regular intervals along the sides of pinnacles, finials, arches, spires, gables and canopies, etc.

CROWS' FEET
Timbered ornamentation used in roofs to surround bosses or to decorate the corners of intersections.

CUSHION CAPITAL
A Norman capital which has the appearance of a flattened cushion. It is in reality a cube of stone with the corners below rounded off.

CUSP
A small projecting point in Gothic tracery whch may be ornamented and is formed by the meeting of two small arches or foils.

DIAGONAL SIDE
(See Cardinal Side).

DOGTOOTH
A pattern of moulding developed and used commonly in the Early English period, consisting of four raised leaves in the shape of a star), a series of the latter being carved in a shallow cavetto round an archway or doorway, etc.

ELLIPTICAL ARCH
A flattened rounded arch of nalf-ellipse shape.

EMBRACED OR ENGAGED TOWER
A west tower connected to the nave by means of an archway, and flanked on its north and south sides by aisles to which access from the tower is provided via two additional archways.

EMBRASURE
One of a series of openings in an embattled or castellated parapet (see Merlon).

FAN-TRACERY
A type of vaulting common in the Perpendicular period, giving the effect of an opened fan.

FILLET
A narrow and usually flat moulding in the form of a narrow band running down a shaft or roll-moulding.

FINIAL
The extended top of a canopy, gable, bench-end, pinnacle, etc., often in the form of a leaf-decoration.

FLEURON
A moulding or ornament consisting of a single decorative flower or other carved foliate object.

FLOWING TRACERY
Ornamental stonework or, occasionally, woodwork of the late Decorated period.

FRIEZE
In Gothic architecture, a decorated horizontal band of stone often located below the parapet of a tower.

GADROONING
Small raised ridges on a surface, the opposite to fluting.

GEOMETRICAL TRACERY
Rib-tracery of the early Decorated period. Placed in window-heads, it usually consists of a combination of circular patterns.

GOTHICK
The name given to the crude imitatory or debased form of Gothic architecture that was introduced in C18, lasting to early C19.

HAMMERBEAM
A short beam projecting horizontally and at right angles, usually from the top of a wall inside a building for the purpose of carrying arch-braces.

HATCHMENT
A large frame of canvas hung on the wall of a church. On this frame is painted the armorial bearings, crests and mottoes, etc., of a deceased person.

HEXAGONAL
Six-sided.

HOODMOULD
(See Label).

INTERSECTING TRACERY
Rib-tracery of the late Early English and early Decorated periods. The tracery pattern is formed when two or more rising mullions divide at the same height into Y-shapes and continue with curves of equal radius until they reach the window-arch. The result is that each main light of the window is shaped like a small lancet window. Y-tracery is a simple type of intersecting tracery.

INTERSTITIUM
The area in a cruciform church between the nave and chancel where the transepts cross at right angles.

JAMBS
The vertical inner sides or faces of a doorway or window.

LABEL
A horizontal hoodmould (projecting stone moulding) over the outside of a doorway or window. The label may possess additional

moulded projections directed downwards, setting the doorway or window in a rectangular frame. Labels were often used in the Perpendicular and following periods.

LANCET WINDOW
A narrow window, typical of the Early English period, having an acutely arched head.

LAUDIAN ALTAR-RAILS
Rails placed round a holy table on three sides. The arrangement stemmed from an order made by Archbishop William Laud in C17.

LEDGER-STONE
A large rectangular flat slab of stone above a grave in the churchyard or within the church. Frequently, ledger-stones may be repositioned standing against walls. Often they are incised with coats of arms or long inscriptions, or have memorial brasses attached to them.

LIERNE-VAULT
A vaulted roof composed of stone or timber which is decorated with lierne ribs, often forming a star-like pattern and characteristic of late C14. By definition, a lierne rib does not arise from a springer or arch-spring and is not a ridge-rib; instead, it intersects a pair of principal ribs.

MERLON
One of a series of raised rectangular sections in an embattled or castellated parapet (see Embrasure).

MISERICORD
A projecting wooden bracket, often carved with comic or grotesque figures, on the underside of a hinged seat of a choir-stall.

MULLION
A slender vertical bar of stone which divides the window-space into two lights. Many windows possess several mullions.

NAILHEAD
A pattern of moulding developed and commonly used in the Early English and late Norman periods. It consists of a series of raised pyramidal shapes.

OCTAGONAL
Eight-sided.

OFFSET (or SET-OFF)
Sloping and stepped part of a buttress or wall, caused by a reduction in thickness of the section immediately above it.

OGEE
A pattern or shape in the form of a double curve, the latter being concave towards one end and convex near the other end (or vice-versa). It was introduced into England c.1310 and was employed extensively in the design of arches, canopies, light-tops, general mouldings, etc., in the Decorated and Perpendicular periods.

PALLADIAN
Descriptive of architectural influences resulting from the work of Andrea Palladio (1508-80) which became prevalent in mid C18. These influences included Roman-style planning, harmonic proportions, symmetry, and good taste.

PARAPET
A low wall to protect any place where there is a drop, such as at the edge of a roof or on the top of a tower. The parapet may be plain, embattled, pierced, panelled or moulded, or a combination of these.

PARCLOSE
A screen which divides a chapel or tomb from the remainder of the church.

PEDESTAL
The upper member of a base which supports a pier, column or shaft. Normally decorated with mouldings, it stands on top of a plinth, the lower member of the base which tends to be plain and square.

PEDIMENT
A low-pitched gable used in classical architecture above portico, doorway, window, monument etc. It may be straight sided (triangular) or curved on its upper side (segmental). An open pediment is one where the centre portion of the sloping or upper sides is left out. A broken pediment is one where the centre portion of the base or cornice is left out. A scrolled (or scrolly) pediment is an open pediment where the ends of the sloping sides terminate in spirals.

PELLET
A pattern of moulding common in Norman times, consisting of raised round discs on a flat band.

PIER
A free-standing upright column, the prime function of which is load-bearing, for instance in an arcade or at the base of a central tower. A pier may be simple in shape (i.e. square, rectangular, round, octagonal, etc.) or composite (for instance, constructed of a set of engaged shafts.)

PILASTER
A shallow rectangular vertical column attached to a wall supporting an arch. Alternatively, its purpose is decorative.

PISCINA
A shallow stone basin, provided with a drain, for washing the holy vessels, normally contained within a niche.

PORTCULLIS
A massive framework of timber and iron used to shut off a gateway at the entrance of a castle or town. A decorative motif of the Perpendicular period.

PUTTO (pl. Putti)
Small naked figure of boy or cherub which may be winged. Is employed as decorative figure on funereal masonry of C17 and C18.

QUADRIPARTITE VAULT
A vaulted roof of which each bay is divided into four triangular sections by means of diagonal ribs which cross at the centre of the span.

QUATREFOIL
A decorative motif frequently used in tracery-work, consisting of four foils or lobes arranged like a four-leaf flower, the foils being in pairs opposite each other and separated by cusps.

QUIRK
A V-shaped or right-angled groove separating two mouldings.

QUOINS
Dressed stones forming the angle or corner of a building to give additional strength.

REREDOS (pl. Reredoses)
Screen or wall behind an altar. Usually ornamented with panelling, niches, pinnacles and statues, etc.

RESPOND
A half-pier attached to a wall. It supports an arch, for instance a chancel arch or arch at the end of an arcade.

RETICULATED TRACERY
Tracery developed and frequently employed in the early Decorated period. It has a regular, net-like shape which may be repeated several times in a window-head, hence the term "reticulation units".

ROOD, ROOD-BEAM, ROOD-LOFT, ROOD-SCREEN
The rood is a cross or crucifix often flanked by figures of Our Lady and St. John set on a timber rood-beam running across the chancel arch of a church. This rood-beam may be partly supported by the rood-loft which is located above the rood-screen. The rood-loft is a gallery with access from the ground-floor via a stairway in an adjoining wall or via a free-standing wooden vice. The rood-screen dividing the chancel from the nave, like the rood-loft front, tends to be highly decorated. Nearly all the medieval roods, rood-beams and rood-lofts were destroyed at the Suppression. However, many rood-screens survive, especially in through-churches, as chancel screens.

RUSTICATION
Ornamental work on quoin stones. The surfaces of these blocks may be deliberately fitted, and the grooved joints between the blocks accentuated. Characteristic of C18.

SALTIRE
Diagonal pattern in the form of St. Andrew's cross, used as a motif in friezes, etc.

SCALLOP
An ornament commonly used in Norman times in the form of a truncated cone which is often repeated round a capital.

SCISSOR-BRACE
One of a pair of straight timbers which cross over in a roof supporting a pair of principal rafters.

SEDILIA (sing. Sedile)
A set of (usually) three seats for an officiating priest and his assistants, recessed in or attached to the south wall of the sanctuary.

SEGMENTAL ARCH
An arch (or pediment) in the shape of the cut-off portion of the circumference of a circle.

SEXPARTITE VAULT
A six-compartmented vaulted roof.

SLYPE
A covered passage-way in a monastic establishment.

SPANDREL
A V-shaped area of walling between two arches, for instance in an arcade below a clerestory. Also, a spandrel is used to describe each of the two triangular areas between an arched doorway and its

rectangular-shaped label. The latter type of spandrel is frequently ornamented.

SPRINGER
The bottom stone of an arch embedded in a pier or wall.

STAR-VAULTING
Vaulting first employed in the early Perpendicular period, in which stellar patterns are made by the use of short lierne-ribs.

STIFF-LEAF FOLIAGE
Stylised carved foliage of the Early English period, used to decorate capitals and bosses.

STOUP
A vessel for holding holy water placed near the entrance of a church, for instance inside or outside a porch. The stoup is usually contained within a niche and may be decorated.

STRING COURSE OR STRING
A horizontal line of projecting stonework internal or external to the building. It may be moulded or ornamented with fleurons, grotesques, etc.

SUBARCUATION
A division of normally one or two mullions at the level of the shoulders of a large early Perpendicular window, the emerging tracery following the curves of the main arch and resulting in the formation of intermediate arches. Within the areas of these intermediate arches and in the areas above them are contained the main lights and tracery-lights of the window.

TRANSOM
A horizontal bar dividing the window area into two tiers of lights.

TREFOIL
A decorative motif frequently used in tracery-work, consisting of three foils or lobes arranged in a circle or in an open configuration and separated by cusps.

TRIFORIUM
An arcaded wall-passage or assembly of blank-arcading above an arcade and below a clerestory.

TUDOR ROSE
A decorative motif often used in the late Perpendicular period on stone and timber, the pattern consisting of a five-petalled flower.

TYMPANUM
This has three meanings:—

1. The area between a door-lintel and the arch above it;
2. The area of a pediment between the cornice and the pediment's upper limits; and
3. The area when filled in between a chancel screen and the roof or arch above it.

VAULT
An arched roof of stone or timber (see Lierne-Vault, Quadripartite Vault, Sexpartite Vault). Alternatively, a burial chamber.

VICE
A spiral staircase which, strictly speaking, winds around a pillar.

VOLUTE
A spiral scroll reminiscent of an Ionic capital, often found in Norman work.

WALL-POST
A vertical piece of timber of short length designed to withstand the downward thrust of a roof.

WATER-HOLDING MOULDING
The hollow between two convex mouldings on a pedestal below a column, pier or shaft. Characteristic of the Early English period.

WAVE
An undulating pattern of moulding consisting of a concave, convex and concave set of contours. Often used on archways, windows and doorways from the first half of C14 onwards, i.e. in Decorated and Perpendicular times.

12. Further Reading on Cheshire Churches

Fred Crossley wrote a series of articles in the 1930s and 40s covering the main architectural periods. These articles are:—

CROSSLEY, F.H. (1938) "Cheshire churches in the twelfth century" in *Journal of the Chester Archaeological Society*[1], Vol. XXXII, Pt. II, pp. 73-97.

CROSSLEY, F.H. (1944) "Church building in Cheshire during the thirteenth century" in *Transactions of the Historic Society of Lancashire and Cheshire*, Vol. 95, pp. 31-41.

CROSSLEY, F.H. (1937) "On the importance of fourteenth century planning in the construction of the churches of Cheshire" in *Journal of the Chester Archaeological Society*, Vol. XXXII, Pt. I, pp. 5-52.

CROSSLEY, F.H. (1940) "The renaissance of Cheshire church building in the late fifteenth and early sixteenth centuries" in *Journal of the Chester Archaeological Society*, Vol. XXXIV, Pt. II, pp. 53-160.

CROSSLEY, F.H. (1942) "Post-reformation church building during the 17th and 18th centuries" in *Journal of the Chester Archaeological Society*, Vol. XXXV, Pt. I, pp. 1-48.

Other articles and a book by the same author include:—

CROSSLEY, F.H. (1936) "Cheshire church towers" in *Journal of the Chester Archaeological Society*, Vol. XXXI, Pt. II, pp. 89-112.

CROSSLEY, F.H. (1943) "Chronological data relating to the churches of Cheshire" in *Transactions of the Lancashire and Cheshire Antiquarian Society*, Vol. LVII, pp. 71-137.

CROSSLEY, F.H. (1949) County Book Series, *Cheshire* (London: Robert Hale), especially Ch. III, "Sandstone building", pp. 158-184.

The "History of Cheshire" series published by the Cheshire Community Council at Chester includes several volumes with information on the historical development of Christianity and church buildings in Cheshire. These volumes are:—

BU'LOCK, J.D. (1972) *Pre-conquest Cheshire, 383 – 1066*, especially Ch. IV, Pt. 3, "Churches and memorials", pp. 75-85.

HUSAIN, B.M.C. (1973) *Cheshire under the Norman earls, 1066 – 1237*, especially Ch. III, Pt. 5, "The Anglo-Norman church", pp. 117-134; and Appendix, "Surviving Norman church building", pp. 135-136.

HEWITT, H.J. (1967) *Cheshire under the three Edwards*, especially Ch. IV, "Building", pp. 48-50 (building materials) and pp. 55-63 (Vale Royal abbey and St. Werburgh's abbey).

DRIVER, J.T. (1971) *Cheshire in the later middle ages, 1399 - 1540,* especially Ch. III, "Buildings", pp. 53-87 (covers the main Perpendicular period of architecture).
BECK, J. (1969) *Tudor Cheshire,* especially Ch. VII, "The Church", pp. 77-95 (the religious upheavals).

Other works which contain material about Cheshire churches are:—

BETHEL, D. (1979) *Portrait of Cheshire* (London: Robert Hale).
BUDDEN, C.W. (1925) *Old English churches, their architecture, furniture and customs as illustrated by the Wirral peninsula* (Liverpool: The Cathedral Bookstall).
CHESTER DIOCESAN HANDBOOK (published annually) Diocesan Office, Chester.
MEE, A. (1968) The King's England series, *Cheshire* (London: Hodder and Stoughton).
MORGAN, P. (ed.) (1978) Domesday Book 26, *Cheshire* (Chichester: Phillimore).
PEVSNER, N. & HUBBARD, E. (1978) The Buildings of England, *Cheshire* (Harmondsworth: Penguin).
RANDALL, D. (1984) *The Search for Old Wirral* (Birkenhead: Countyvise).
RICHARDS, R. (1973) *Old Cheshire churches* (Manchester: Morten).
SYLVESTER, D. (1967) "Parish and township in Cheshire and North-East Wales" in *Journal of the Chester Archaeological Society,* Vol. 54, pp.23-35.
SYLVESTER, D. (1980) The Darwen County History Series, *A history of Cheshire* (Chichester: Phillimore).

Additional sources of information may be found in:—

HARRIS, B.E. (ed.) (1983) *The history of the county palatine of Chester,* A short bibliography and guide to sources (Chester: Cheshire Community Council).

---

[1]The Society has changed its name several times since it was founded. This is its present name.

Appendix: Arch Shapes

The shape of an arch is defined in terms of the number and position of the centres of circles, the segments of which circles collectively form the boundary of the arch. The chief shapes are shown in the accompanying diagram.

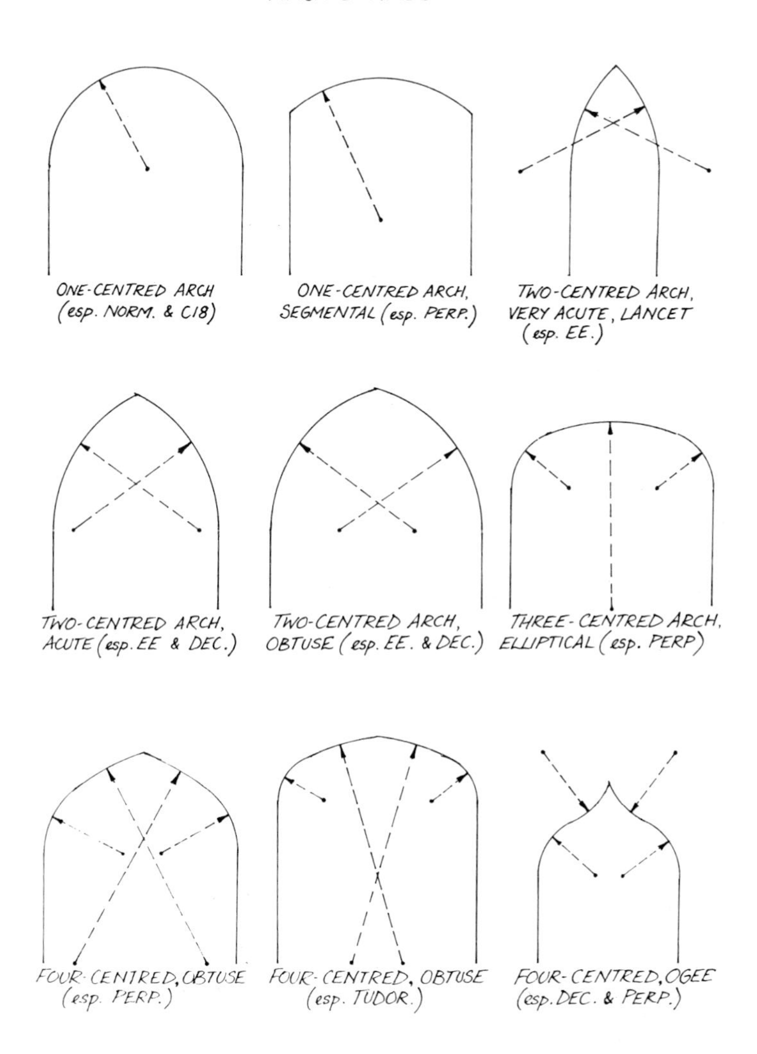

OTHER TITLES FROM

Local History

Birkenhead Priory....Jean McInniss
Birkenhead Park....Jean McInniss
The Spire is Rising....Dorothy Harden
The Search for Old Wirral....David Randall
Neston and Parkgate....Jeffrey Pearson
Scotland Road....Terry Cooke
Helen Forrester Walk....K. Rickard
Women at War....Pat Ayres
Merseyside Moggies....R.M. Lewis
Dream Palaces....Harold Ackroyd
Forgotten Shores....Maurice Hope
Cheshire Churches....Roland W. Morant
Storm over the Mersey....Beryl Wade
Memories of Heswall 1935 — 1985....Heswall W.E.A.

Local Railway Titles

Seventeen Stations to Dingle....John W. Gahan
The Line Beneath the Liners....John W. Gahan
Steel Wheels to Deeside....John W. Gahan
Seaport to Seaside....John W. Gahan
Northern Rail Heritage....K. Powell and G. Body
A Portrait of Wirral's Railways....Roger Jermy

Local Shipping Titles

Sail on the Mersey....Michael Stammers
Ghost Ships on the Mersey....K.J. Williams
The Liners of Liverpool - *Part I*....Derek Whale
The Liners of Liverpool - *Part II*....Derek Whale
The Liners of Liverpool - *Part III*....Derek Whale
Hands off the Titanic....Monica O'Hara
Mr. Merch and other stories....Ken Smith

Local Sport

The Liverpool Competition (Local Cricket)....P.N. Walker
Lottie Dod....Jeffrey Pearson

History with Humour

The One-Eyed City....Rod Mackay
Hard Knocks....Rod Mackay
The Binmen are coming....Louis Graham

Natural History

Birdwatching in Cheshire....Eric Hardy

Other Titles

Speak through the Earthquake, Wind & Fire....Graham A. Fisher
It's Me, O Lord....Members of Heswall Churches
Companion to the Fylde....R.K. Davies
Country Walks on Merseyside....David Parry
A-Z Cheshire Ghosts....Muriel Armand